GARDENING TIME

VEGETABLE GROWING

ARTHUR BILLITT

CENTRAL

Boxtree

First published in Great Britain in 1988 by Boxtree Limited

Copyright © Central Independent Television plc 1988

ISBN 1 85283 226 6

Line drawings by Mei Lim
Designed by Groom and Pickerill
Typeset by York House Typographic
Printed in Italy by New Interlitho spa, Milan
for Boxtree Limited
36 Tavistock Street
London
WC2E 7PB

The author and publishers would like to thank Sutton Seeds Ltd
for use of photographs on pp 53, 60, 64, 79, 80, 90

CONTENTS

PREFACE

The Gardening Time programme was started in 1972 as a weekly feature and since then has continued to be produced 52 weeks of the year.

The garden is situated in a Birmingham park in the suburb of Kings Heath. The first two presenters of the programme, Cyril Fletcher and the late Bob Price, created from a piece of waste ground a superb garden of just over one-third of an acre which contained a rockery, waterfall and pool, island beds, paved areas, a small vegetable garden, a small soft fruit garden and the typical 8 × 20 greenhouse.

In 1983, the City of Birmingham Parks and Amenities Department gave permission to extend the garden to 7 acres. Work began on an adjacent site and to date we have created over 1½ acres of new gardens with different styles of landscape. There is also an extended vegetable garden with organic and non-organic trial bed areas, a large herb garden and trial beds for roses, dahlias, chrysanthemums and bedding plants – all propagated from three new greenhouses.

The four expert presenters of the Gardening Time programme are Arthur Billitt (fruit and vegetables), Jock Davidson (house plants), Geoff Amos (all-round gardening, especially bedding plants) and Howard Drury (alpines, conifers, heathers, shrubs) who is also the programme's Horticultural Adviser.

The programme spans the entire year and these accompanying books show how, by doing the right things at the right time, anybody can become a successful gardener.

JOHN PULLEN
PRODUCER

INTRODUCTION

Although it lacks the colour, a well-tended vegetable garden can be as attractive as a flower garden. And the rewards for the effort put in are considerable. It offers the challenge of growing crops really well, and provides the satisfaction of raising fresher and better vegetables than can be bought in shops. Unlike the commercial grower, the home gardener is able to concentrate on growing varieties for quality, with particular emphasis on flavour, which is so sadly absent in most mass-produced vegetables, where damage-free transport, shelf life and eye appeal are far more important.

Home-grown vegetables have the extra quality of freshness, retaining all the natural vitamins and minerals so often lost during commercial storage. Furthermore, the all-year-round exercise involved in growing vegetables is in itself a contributory factor to good health. Indeed, there are few more enjoyable occupations.

ARTHUR BILLITT

As a handy cross-reference for calculating plant dimensions, planting depths and distances, etc., where mentioned in the text, the following list gives approximate metric equivalents to imperial measurements.

½ in	1 cm	18 in	45 cm
1 in	2.5 cm	20 in	50 cm
2 in	5 cm	24 in	60 cm
3 in	7.5 cm	30 in	75 cm
4 in	10 cm	36 in	90 cm
5 in	13 cm	4 ft	1.2 m
6 in	15 cm	5 ft	1.5 m
7 in	18 cm	6 ft	1.8 m
8 in	20 cm	7 ft	2.1 m
9 in	23 cm	8 ft	2.4 m
10 in	25 cm	9 ft	2.7 m
11 in	28 cm	10 ft	3 m
12 in	30 cm	12 ft	3.6 m
15 in	38 cm	15 ft	4.5 m

1. THE FAMILY-SIZED VEGETABLE PLOT

Space nowadays is at a premium. Although many rented allotments may measure, say, 90 ft x 30 ft (27 m x 9 m), this is far too large for average family needs. Indeed, with careful planning, using the best varieties of vegetables and by intercropping where possible, an area of 20 ft x 10 ft (6 m x 3 m) can supply almost all the fresh vegetables needed for two people throughout the season. For the larger family, of course, this area should be increased accordingly.

Apart from the fact that an over-large plot may result in a glut of produce, it is far better to maintain a smaller, well-cared for area with continuous weed and pest control.

Choosing the site
The vegetable garden needs to be kept in first-class condition and carefully sited. Too often it is treated as a 'Cinderella', either screened from view by a hedge or positioned in shade under trees. A hedge is acceptable provided it does not cast a shadow on the vegetables for long periods of the day; but it is impossible to grow vegetables satisfactorily in continuous shade. Another point to remember is the distance between the growing area and the kitchen. The closer it is to the house, the more frequently you will tend it, checking on the various crops as they come ready for use. And you can pop in and out conveniently, even if it is raining.

Once you have decided on the site and size of the vegetable garden, make sure you have a path to approach it and wholly

A well-tended vegetable garden.

10

surround it. The latter will, ensure, in the case of a small plot, that there is seldom any need to step on the soil when picking sprouts or lifting root crops such as carrots and parsnips during not-so-dry autumn and winter conditions.

Tools for the job

It is very important to choose the right tools, which should be well made, strong but as light as possible. When buying a spade, make sure that it feels balanced in your hands, that the shaft is smooth (preferably made of ash), and that there are no rough or sharp edges where it is fitted into the spade itself. Get one with a forged steel blade, which will last a lifetime, especially if you clean it and give it a wipe with an oily rag after use. Stainless steel spades look good and are more expensive, but are also slightly heavier. Spades are made in three sizes, but you don't have to buy

the largest – it won't necessarily help you to get more digging done in a given time. A spade fitted with a T handle is good value but in these days of plastic handles it is not always easy to find one in the shops or garden centres.

A good garden fork is also essential and here the same basic standards apply. A full-sized fork is ideal for the heavier jobs such as digging the potatoes, spreading compost, etc., but a smaller border fork will do equally well and is easier for women to handle.

A power driven cultivator is an unnecessary expense, certainly for a small vegetable garden. No machine does the job as well as a spade.

Surface cultivation between the rows and the plants during the growing season is all-important. It controls the weeds, allows air to enter the soil, which is good for root activity, and also creates a surface tilth which restricts the loss of soil moisture during dry weather. This job requires the use of a hoe. There are many types available, from the old long-handled draw hoe to the latest Wolf double-edged hoe, which is a great improvement on the standard type of Dutch hoe. For hoeing between rows of crops such as onions, where considerable care is needed, a short-handled swan-necked onion hoe is ideal; these are available in various blade widths (Spear & Jackson 3-5 in, Wolf also 2 in). For seed-bed or planting preparations in the spring you will need a three-pronged cultivator (Wolf, several sizes) to break down the roughly dug soil. A 12 in rake (Wolf or Spear & Jackson) is a must; both these makes are practical and strong. A garden line (Spear & Jackson) will ensure that the rows are always straight, or you can easily make one yourself. For planting leeks and brassicas there is nothing better than a dibber (available with a T handle), but for other jobs a garden trowel is usually better.

To give the plants a good start, buy a watering can with a long spout and a removable fine rose, the latter for seed-bed watering. Sooner or later, too, spraying will be necessary. Hozelock-ASL markets a wide range of reliable sprayers.

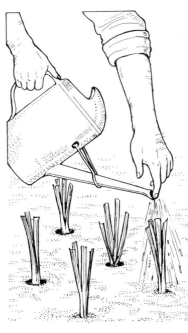

Dribbling in water to wash soil roots of newly planted leeks.

12

2. Soil Types and How to Improve Them

There are basically four types of soil: light sandy, medium loam, heavy clay and chalky; but within these groups there are many mixtures, all of which can be improved and made more productive by regular and good cultivation practices. On light sandy soils, which are free-draining and dry out rapidly in warm weather, fertilisers are best applied at lower dose rates than normal, but more frequently. Applications of well-rotted farmyard manure or compost to improve the moisture- and nutrient-holding capacity should be regular and liberal, since these break down much more quickly in light sandy soils than in any other type of soil.

Light soils

Practically all light soils, especially those with a little natural peat in their make-up or those improved by the addition of compost, etc., are inclined to be on the acid side. So for most vegetables, with the exception of potatoes, it is wise to make an annual pre-sowing or planting pH level check. A reading below pH 6 would indicate the need for an application of garden lime.

Light soils, apart from draining well, warm up earlier in the spring and are capable of producing earlier crops than the heavier soils. Medium loam types of soil (mixtures of sand and clay) are regarded as the best for vegetable growing and easy to work.

Heavy soils

Heavy soils with differing amounts of clay in their make-up vary considerably, from those that are not too difficult to cultivate to the frustrating brick clay type, which, unless handled properly, is sticky in winter and rock hard in summer. Yet the soil nutrient levels are high, as are the cropping potentials. Late autumn or early winter is the time to turn the ground over to the full depth of the spade, leaving large rough clods exposed to the weather. Without the help of nature – the frost to separate the clay particles followed by March winds to dry them out – seed-bed preparation is virtually impossible; but pre-Christmas digging pays real dividends. For heavy soils, digging in some compost or farmyard manure, slightly strawy rather than completely rotted, helps to keep the soil more open, improving root systems. Too much well-rotted compost or manure can increase the slug population, whereas the incorporation of well-weathered ashes tends to reduce it, and helps to make the clay easier to manage.

These same treatments improve chalky soils, but here too the real answer begins with winter digging and ends with breaking the flaking clods down in spring. Never re-dig before sowing or planting, as this will undo all your good work.

3. DRAINAGE AND WATERING

With the possible exception of celery and celeriac, our more commonly grown crops quickly display their dislike of badly drained or waterlogged soils, which results in poor or non-existent root activity. A few inches of water cover soon causes plant death, so in higher rainfall areas and in low lying valleys, or on heavy clay soils, efficient drainage is essential. On light sandy or medium-type soils overlying gravel, natural drainage works well, especially when the ground slopes slightly downhill. But to improve the drainage of heavy clay soils, some form of underground channelling is required, not always practical when your plot is surrounded by neighbours' properties.

Building a drain

The best method is to lay 3 in land drains or brick rubble in slightly downhill-sloping trenches 2 ft deep and, say, 12 ft apart, preferably covered with washed gravel or rubble. This works well when the channels are linked together at the lower end or side of the plot, with a continuing fall beyond. Without such means of disposal a deep sump filled with rubble might suffice except in difficult deep clays. Ridging or mounting may be necessary with a combination of boggy soil and heavy rainfall, although this entails a good deal of extra effort. If this is done

during the winter, the vertical sides should remain intact for a whole season. The greater the waterlogging, the higher the mounds need to be. The width of the mounds at the top is important, 2-3 ft is a good growing width, with a trench about 12 in wide between each mound.

On plots where winter water is an insoluble problem, it is best to concentrate solely on spring and summer cropping. Rough-dig the ground before Christmas, wait for March with its drying winds, and break up the crust with a three-pronged cultivator.

Keeping the plants moist

In spring and summer the problem is reversed. Plants must have a certain amount of water if they are to be healthy, especially when the weather turns hot and dry. Seeds need moisture in the soil to germinate; so if an opened seed drill is dry, water it before sowing. After germination, the seedlings will have shallow roots, and in drought conditions they may be at risk. Water them thoroughly in the evening with a fine rose on the can. Just sprinkling water on the surface to lay the dust is worse than no water at all, since the fibrous roots need to delve down for moisture.

This golden rule for thorough watering applies as well to established plants. If you have means for collecting rainwater, use it in preference to mains water.

14

4. GETTING THE GROUND READY

The ideal time to begin preparing the site is in early autumn, but certainly before Christmas. If you are starting from scratch with a plot of virgin soil that has not been cultivated within recent years, avoid the common mistake of cleaning away and burning the top covering of rough grass and mixture of perennial and annual weeds, for these will have provided the soil with a store of natural plant nutrients. Start by digging a trench at one end of the plot, the width and depth of a full-size spade. Carry the dug-out clods, complete with grass and weeds, to the far end of the plot where they will be needed

Dig a trench the width and depth of a full-size spade.

Ensure any vegetation is well-covered with soil.

Trench for planting potatoes.

for filling in the final length of trenching. Having opened the trench, start digging to the full depth of the spade, turning over each spadeful completely, so that the grass and weeds are at the bottom. Then as you progress row by row, make sure that all the vegetation is well and truly covered by soil.

Removing the weeds
With the plot well dug, frost, wind and rain will play their part; and in early spring, when the soil begins to warm up, weed and grass seeds will germinate and perennial weed roots start to shoot. Now is the time to get them out, using the three-pronged cultivator to break up the top few inches and the hoe to cut off the weeds. Make this a weekly routine, and don't start sowing until you have completely beaten the weeds.

Land that has been growing grass and weeds for years is inclined to be acid and short of calcium, so check the pH level; if it is below pH 6 an application of garden lime will benefit all vegetable crops with the exception of potatoes.

The neglected patch
If you are taking over a neglected vegetable garden or allotment, the soil is likely to be deficient in natural fertility. Again the best time to start putting matters right is in the autumn. Winter digging, with compost or farmyard manure incorporated at the right time, will soon bring life and fertility back to exhausted soils. Go carefully with potatoes and brassicas until you are certain that neither potato eelworm or clubroot are lying in wait. Either of these problems could be the reason for the previous owner's neglect or decision to quit.

5. PREPARING AND SOWING SEED-BEDS

Whilst outside seed sowing takes place during the growing season, normally in the spring or early summer, the degree of success achieved is determined by the preparation work done well in advance, in the autumn. Start by deeply and roughly turn over over the soil, digging to the depth of the spade, and breaking up with a fork any hard pan underneath, as this is often the cause of unshapely root crops, particularly carrots and parsnips. With the roughly dug clods exposed to the weather, the process of seed-bed preparation goes on unaided throughout the winter.

With the arrival of spring, wait, if possible, for a day when the soil is dry. On heavy soil you may need to stand on a plank, for compaction of soil is fatal if you want a first-class seed-bed. But after the March winds have dried out the top, even the heaviest clay, thanks to the frost, will break down the first time you go through it with the three-pronged cultivator. If the weather stays fine, spread the job over a period of three days, twice through with the cultivator to continue the breakdown and drying process, and finally with a garden rake, levelling the area and creating a fine dry top soil tilth.

Sowing

All is now ready for sowing with confidence, but do remember the wise gardener's maxim: 'Sow dry, plant wet'. To ensure that every seed drill is straight and well separated from the next, use a garden line (home-made with a length of cord and two short canes or bought ready-made). For small seed-beds, however, a thin piece of straight wood is easier to handle. Then draw out a drill along the whole length of the line or wood, using the corner of a rake.

Drawing a drill for outdoor sowing, using a garden line.

Make sure that the drill is very shallow when sowing small seeds such as carrots or lettuce; they should only just be covered with fine soil when sowing is complete. Sowing seeds too deeply is a common cause of failure and complaints about germination. In fact, seed sown beyond its natural depth does not germinate, but simply stays put and rots. Another important point, especially with carrots and onions, is to sow the seed thinly along the drill. This saves much difficult thinning out after germination and avoids eventual pest problems.

Having sown the seed carefully, take the rake to one end of the drill and draw it lightly along, following the garden line to the other end. Never rake across a seed-bed, which may shift the seed sideways. Before moving the line on for the next row, go along the drill with the head of the rake down, lightly settling the dry tilth; but on no account do this if the top soil is moist. And finally, don't forget to label the row.

6. TRANSPLANTING

It is often more convenient and more satisfactory to sow certain vegetables in one place and to grow the plants up to a stage or size when they can be safely moved from their pots or seed-bed to be transplanted into their final growing positions. Brassica plants, for example, can be grown in small seed-beds if there are no vacant spaces available on the main vegetable plot. Indeed, more often than not, brassicas benefit from a move; the tap roots are broken and this encourages the development of more and more fibrous roots, giving the plants extra vigour and better anchorage. Do not, however, transplant brassicas until they measure about 5-6 in. Water the seed-bed generously, especially in dry weather, before lifting the plants with a fork so as to ease them out with the maximum amount of root. For brassicas to settle down well after transplanting, the ground should be fairly firm, not recently dug; and for planting, a dibber is better than a trowel.

Measuring the distance

The planting distances between the plants and between the rows vary according to the ultimate size of the plants. For brussels sprouts, sprouting broccoli, etc., 30 in each way will not be too much; for cauliflowers it should be slightly less, and for small to medium-size cabbages 20 in each way may be sufficient. A distance of 12 in is often recommended for small calabrese spears intended for freezing, but they are better given more room. The distance can be gauged by making knots in the garden line; then it is just a dibber hole at each knot. If the ground is dry, place a little water in each dibber hole, and after this

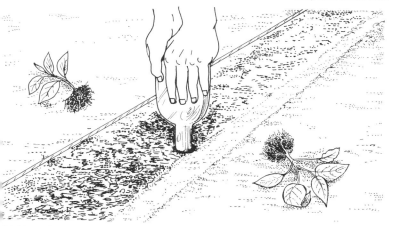

Making a hole with a dibber for transplanting brassicas.

has soaked in, set the plants just a fraction deeper than previously in the seed-bed. Finally, use the heel of the gardener's boot to firm the soil carefully around the stem, and for good measure add some extra water in the heel mark.

Pot plants
Plants grown in peat pots (see page 22) should be planted without the removal of the pots, but in most cases the rims of the pots must be below ground level, otherwise the enclosed compost quickly dries out. Lettuce thinnings can be transplanted up to midsummer. Since the lettuce will mature three or four weeks later, this will help to maintain continuity of supply. When transplanting pot-grown plants such as tomatoes, marrows, etc., outside, it is wise to add some well rotted compost to the planting hole; this will ensure that they are less likely to suffer a shortage of water until they are well established.

7. Greenhouse and Cloches

A small greenhouse, even if it is unheated, affords sufficient protection to start sowing vegetable seed long before the open ground outside has either started to dry out or lose its winter chill. The combined use of a greenhouse and a row or two of cloches, the former to get the seed germinated and plants ready for transplanting, the latter in position outside to coddle them for a while, is an ideal arrangement. It is then possible to bring forward the cropping and harvesting dates of peas, broad beans runner beans, lettuce, beetroot, cauliflowers, etc.

Germination of such seeds as tomatoes, cucumbers, marrows, peppers, sweetcorn, etc., requires an extra level of temperature. Heating the whole greenhouse is expensive, but the problem can be solved by using a Ward propagating frame, large enough to take three half-size and four quarter-size seed trays or eight half-pots. This is electrically heated but economical, the

Dwarf broad beans and radishes under cloche.

temperature controlled by a thermostat fitted with a small dial at the end of the frame. Just above 60°F (15°C) is the right temperature for most vegetable seeds to achieve good early germination. If heat is not available, however, timing of tender subjects such as tomatoes is important; this should not be earlier than April, otherwise they will suffer a setback on the greenhouse bench after pricking out.

The unheated greenhouse

By March the days are lengthening and some warmth from the sunlight will filter into the greenhouse and be stored in the soil for release during the night. Now is the time to sow lettuce – a couple of seeds in each small peat pot will ensure that after germination the strongest seedling can be selected and the surplus discarded. You will also be able to sow Little Marvel peas, a variety full of flavour and sweetness, as well as broad beans (try 'The Sutton' instead of the flavourless 'Aquadulce'). For a few early cauliflowers 'All the Year Round' takes a lot of beating. And runner beans, sown in mid-April, produce strong plants by the end of May or early June, just the right time to plant them out after the last spring frosts. All these and more can be started in small peat pots, which should be thoroughly damped in warm water before being filled with seed compost. Some peat pots (Fyba Pots) come with a trace of fertilisers in the peat, excellent for ensuring robust plants by the time they go outside.

Cloches

To get the best results from cloches, put them out in a line well in advance of planting, so that the covered soil has time to lose some of its chill and wetness. For lettuce and beetroot, small tent cloches are sufficient, whilst for peas, beans and cauliflowers, the larger barn cloches will be needed. Because the sun's warmth is increasing daily, small gaps should be left between each cloche, otherwise the plants may get cooked. The cloches can be removed for periodic surface cultivation, which is good for the plants and for weed control, or for watering during a very dry spring. Most makes of cloches are provided with a pair of ends to prevent the cold winds being tunnelled along the row.

8. CROP ROTATION

A crop rotation plan is essential for preventing eventual problems from soil-borne pests and diseases. By making certain that no one crop is grown on the same spot more than once in three years, pests and diseases are deprived of their host plants for at least two seasons, time enough, one hopes, for them to die of starvation.

In a three-yearly crop rotation system, vegetables can be divided roughly into three groups: brassicas (cabbage, brussels sprouts, etc.), root crops (onions, carrots, parsnips, etc.), and potatoes plus legumes (peas, beans, etc.). Although not ideal, it is a practical approach when only one or two rows of potatoes are grown.

Earthing up potatoes.

The importance of crop rotation

The main reason why crop rotation is so necessary for continuous successful vegetable growing on a plot is that no two groups of plants take up nutrients and trace elements from the soil in the same ratio; so without a change of crop the soil nutrient levels are liable to become unbalanced. Another factor, perhaps not fully understood, is the difference in excreted waste from plant to plant. The more serious soil pests and diseases are related to individual groups of plants and do not attack vegetable plants outside the group. Potato eelworm, for example, is confined to potatoes and tomatoes, both members of the same family. And clubroot, which attacks brassicas, often results from the neglect of crop rotation.

A practical plan

Divide the vegetable growing area in to roughly three equal-sized sections. Having established the measurements of the plot, the plant develops as follows:-

First year
Section A: root crops i.e. carrots, parsnips, etc.
Section B: brassicas i.e. cabbages, etc.
Section C: legumes i.e. peas, beans, etc.
Second year
Section A: brassicas.
Section B: peas and beans.
Section C: root crops.
Third year
Section A: peas and beans.
Section B: rootcrops.
Section C: brassicas.

In the fourth year it is back to the cropping plan as for the first year.

There is scope here for variations and additions. Thus a row of quick-maturing 'Fortune' lettuce can be squeezed in alongside the first row of early peas and there will be room for a few radishes in the brassica section particularly as they are members of the same family. And when the early peas are cleared there will be a gap for more lettuce such as 'Little Gem'. Take advantage of empty spaces but do not overcrowd or break crop rotation rules.

9. CATCH CROPPING AND INTERCROPPING

Radish 'Cherry Belle'.

Catch cropping is a way of making maximum use of limited growing space by sowing seed of some of the quicker maturing crops between rows of the slower moving ones. Salad crops such as lettuce and radishes are obvious subjects for the job. Seed of first lettuces 'Fortune' and radishes 'Cherry Belle' can be sown in a separate rows 6 in apart, then covered with small tent cloches. The radishes take up little space and are ready for pulling in roughly six weeks, while the lettuces are just beginning to spread their leaves out and will quickly heart up, provided the spacing between the cloches is increased for ventilation.

The next opportunity for catch cropping comes with the sowing of first rows of early peas and broad beans, neither of which grow very rapidly nor exceed a final height of 18 in. By this time of year the soil is beginning to warm up and the growing climate generally much better. Half a row of either lettuce or radishes will probably be sufficient. This time try sowing 'Little Gem', a crisp small cos lettuce. Alternatively you could try the onion 'White Lisbon' for pulling green as spring onions; some will still be in good condition after the peas and beans are cleared away. The traditional celery trench, with its heaped up soil either side, provides a golden opportunity for catch cropping with lettuce and radishes: before sowing just top the ridges with a rake and maybe water afterwards if the weather is dry. Or they will do equally well in June when you plant out your widely spaced brussels sprouts. Both crops will mature before the brassica foliage meets in the rows. The point to remember is that light and air are just as essential as moisture to the success of catch crops.

The same could be said for intercropping potatoes with brassicas, not as commonly practised as it was before the importance of 'crop rotation' was fully understood, and when potatoes were grown with more space between each row. To be successful for a single season, the potatoes need to be planted in rows 3 ft apart, otherwise the brussels sprouts, etc., planted in June between the potato ridges, soon become smothered with potato foliage. In the long term such intercropping is likely to violate crop rotation rules, which could result in club root on brassicas raising its ugly head.

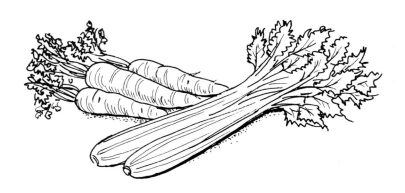

10. Work in the Growing Season

Inadequate attention to weed control during the growing season will quickly transform a vegetable garden into a jungle of weeds. The first job is to stop the initial weed onslaught in early spring, breaking up the top soil two or three times in succession with the three-pronged cultivator. This is perhaps the most important surface cultivation of the whole year.

Weed-free soil is essential for seed sowing, otherwise there could be a growth race between the weed and the vegetable seedlings. Great care is needed when cultivating and weeding in and between the rows of small seedlings such as carrots and onions; at that stage weed seedlings within the row are best removed by hand, but the swan-necked onion hoe is more efficient between the rows. Allow the hoe to cut the weeds off without the blade penetrating more than a quarter or half-inch into the soil. Later on, when the seedlings are larger, a Dutch-type hoe will do a similar job without the need to bend down so low. Hoeing also creates a tilth of fine, slightly disturbed soil, which reduces moisture losses, important during a dry season, and allows air to penetrate the soil, thus stimulating root activity and growth.

Cultivating between the stronger free-standing crops such as brassicas is somewhat easier. Again the Dutch-type hoe does the weed control job well and it is also useful for incorporating the occasional fertiliser application. As and when some of the earlier crops such as peas and beans are cleared away, make sure that the ground is free of weeds before sowing or planting the following crop. Go over the cleared ground first with a hoe and then with a cultivator, not going too deep to avoid excess loss of moisture. Cultivations amongst crops should also be shallow, otherwise roots could be damaged; parsnips cut with a hoe start to rot as do onions.

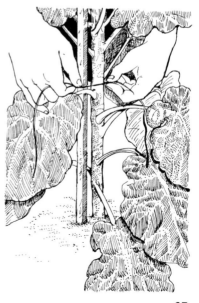

Staking Brussels sprouts.

27

11. FERTILISERS

Whilst well-rotted compost and farmyard manure applied regularly to a vegetable plot certainly help to maintain the fertility and health of the soil, crop yields can be increased considerably by the discreet use of fertilisers. Generally the best results are obtained from the application of so-called balanced fertilisers, in other words those that have nitrogen (N), phosphates (P) and potash (K) in their formulations. Nitrogen encourages leaf growth, phosphates aid root and seed development, whereas potash ensures healthy growth and at the same time improves vegetable flavour. Balanced fertilisers may be based entirely on inorganic ingredients, for example 'Growmore', which has long been popular with vegetable growers. One hundred per cent organic formulations are available but usually at a higher price; these are slower acting but contain minor or trace elements not present in inorganic fertilisers. And then there are fertiliser mixtures on the markets with both organic and inorganic constituents, such as the PBI 'Back to Nature'.

Regular feeding

It is at the beginning of the season when the winter dug soil is being broken down for seedbed or planting preparations that we get the best value from balanced fertiliser applications, worked in with a rake at 2 oz to the square yard (60 g per m^2). For follow-up surface applications between the rows of growing crops, half the pre-sowing rate is sufficient. Granular or dry fertiliser formulations applied during the growing season are more effective and act more quickly when lightly hoed in and followed up with a watering when the weather is dry.

Leafy crops, brassicas in particular, sometimes need a tonic, especially in the spring or early summer to get them going. Nitrogen alone is suitable for the job. Here again the choice can be inorganic i.e. sulphate of ammonia, nitro chalk or nitrate of soda, at no more than 1 oz to the square yard (30 g per m^2) around the plants, or organic, dried blood being an excellent alternative.

Other straight fertilisers are super phosphate of lime, freely available, basic slag with its trace elements (not so easy to find these days), and sulphate of potash, sometimes used on its own when plants are making excessive amounts of leaf growth.

Foliar fertilisers, applied either as a spray or watered on to the foliage, are quick acting, some of the nutrients being taken up in part by the leaves, a useful emergency treatment which should be applied in the late evening during hot, dry weather in the summer.

28

Acidity and alkalinity

Whilst garden lime is not a fertiliser in the true sense of the word, the calcium it supplies enables plants to make better use of other nutrients, particularly phosphates. Its application improves the texture of heavy clay soils, making them easier to work. Continual vegetable cropping, plus repeated applications of compost or farmyard manure, tend to make light and medium soils progressively more acid, a condition which slowly reduces yields in most crops, with the possible exception of potatoes. For continuous brassica growing, with its consequent risk of clubroot, the soil should be somewhere near or slightly below neutral pH 7. The degree of acidity or alkalinity in a soil can be determined by the use of a simple soil testing kit or pH meter. For soils below pH 6 apply 3 oz to the square yard (90 g per m^2) of garden lime, but never before planting potatoes. And be particularly careful not to over-lime, as it can produce problems.

12. Harvesting and Storing

Vegetables gathered at just the right time can be stored naturally or, in many cases, by deep freezing, for use months later in the kitchen. Nature, however, makes its own provision for over-winter storage and the survival of the species, which involves either the production of seed (peas, beans, etc.) or roots to remain in the ground to produce seedheads the following season (parsnips, carrots, etc.). Vegetables in this latter group store much better if left in the ground and lifted as required, or stored in clamps.

Root crops should never be stored in plastic bags, for they will invariably rot. On well-drained soils, where slugs are not a problem, a winter hardy variety of carrot such as 'Autumn King' is best left in the ground; carrots stored in sand or peat often shrivel, rot or go mouldy. Parsnips are certainly best left in the row; frost improves the flavour but it is a good idea to lift a few at a time during the winter and leave them on top in case the soil is frozen when they are wanted. Potatoes are frost-sensitive, and lifting at the end of the season for clamping is advisable. Beetroot and celeriac will stand a little amount of frost but clamping is wiser.

Clamping
For small quantities of vegetables, a mixed clamp is practical, requiring only a limited area of bare ground and a base covering of straw, on which the potatoes, etc., should be heaped, taking care not to bruise. Then cover the heap with a good layer of straw, cone-fashion, with a protruding wisp for ventilation, and bury the clamp under a deep layer of soil. The depth of straw and soil will depend on the likely severity of frost.

Onions and shallots need special care, for they must be mature, with the foliage dried off naturally, usually towards the end of August or early September. After lifting, lay them out to dry in the sunshine, and then string them up as a rope or with the dry tops removed hung in a large mesh net, storing

them in a place where there is good air movement and freedom from frost. Fully ripe marrows will keep for several months hung up in open nets in a frost-free shed. Haricot beans and peas can be harvested ripe and dried for winter use.

Freezing

Home freezers have brought a new dimension to storing surplus vegetables, but the secret is always to pick the crops whilst still in peak condition and to get them into the freezer immediately after harvesting while they are still crisp and fresh. Some vegetable varieties freeze better than others – a quality usually noted on the seed packet. For the best results and freezing techniques, be guided by a specialist book on the subject.

(Above) Carrots for harvesting can be eased up wih a fork.
(Below) Harvesting potatoes.

13. COMPOST MAKING

Some people question the need for compost making. After all, why not simply burn garden rubbish? But there is a good reason for this extra trouble. In nature, trees shed their leaves annually and many plants grow and die during the season, thereby returning to the soil the nutrients collected during their lifetime. This recurring cycle of events maintains an almost constant level of soil fertility and health in the undisturbed plant world. But when we start vegetable growing, removing crops for use in the kitchen and perhaps burning the rest of the plant material, we seriously interfere with nature's fertility plan. So by making a compost heap we are simply abiding by nature's well established rules.

The secret of successful compost making is to allow nature's contributors, soil bacteria, soil fungi and earthworms, to play their part, so that the finished product, humus, is friable and crumbly. Any green garden material can be used, but seed-bearing weeds should be avoided, since the heat generated is never enough to destroy them.

A circular compost container, made of chicken wire or plastic and supported by wooden stakes.

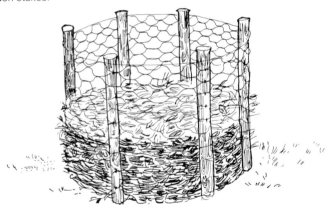

Bins and containers

A compost heap needs sidewall protection to keep everything compact and tidy. One cheap solution to this problem is a 4 ft circle or square of 1 in mesh chicken wire, supported by four stakes or strong canes.

Wooden slatted bins are more expensive but more durable, in handy sizes of say 5 ft square and 4 ft high. Two of these, joined by slats at the back may be set 5 ft apart. The centre open-fronted space is useful for short-time storage of autumn leaves, etc., at a time when the bins are full of well rotted compost awaiting clearance. Some of the expensive plastic compost containers are not too successful in use, but one reliable type marketed by Auriol consists of a lightweight plastic-covered wire frame which holds a large bottomless plastic bag fitted with holes. When full, the bag is tied and left for the process to continue: the frame is removed and can be set up again to support another bag.

Making the compost

Whatever type of container is used, the basic rules for good compost making are the same. Start by placing the first layer of green material (the more mixed the better) on bare soil this allows the earthworms access. Treat alternate 8 in layers with either a handful of garden lime (the sweet-ener) or a handful of ordinary garden soil to start the build-up of soil bacteria and soil fungi. Air is essential for the decomposition – hence the spaces between the slats and the holes in the plastic bags – each layer must be compressed, especially around the sides of the bin. The compost needs no special protection from the weather, nor does it have to be turned. Addition of sulphate of ammonia or a proprietary compost maker, in place of garden lime, will accelerate the breakdown processes.

If the starting material contains a large proportion of lawn mowings, use extra garden lime plus a proprietary compost maker as additives, otherwise the end product could turn out to be more soggy than friable. When emptying a bin, use the top, partially decomposed layer to start the next one.

14. THE VEGETABLE GARDEN IN WINTER

Even in the dull, cold winter months there are usually some brighter and milder periods when a spell outside is always good for the garden. Winter is the best time to prepare the ground for the next season's growing, and also the time to

reap some of the benefits of last year's activities. There will be frost-hardy crops still standing on the ground awaiting the call from the kitchen for fresh home grown vegetables, including perhaps winter brassicas such as the extra-late brussels sprout 'Troika', the great winter cabbage, 'January King', the curly kale 'Dwarf Green Curled', which survives the severest conditions, and a couple of rows of purple sprouting and white sprouting broccoli. As the winter progresses, some of the bottom leaves of the brassicas turn yellow, and these should be periodically removed, firstly to keep the plants clean and secondly to provide a little more material for the compost heap.

At the beginning of the winter roughly one-third of the vegetable garden will still be carrying crops; the rest will be vacant, already dug or waiting for the spade and the weather. Rough digging the ground to the full depth of the spade is particularly useful at the time, so that the frozen water in the clods can later break down the clay. Before digging the area where your peas, beans and potatoes are to go, spread some well-rotted compost. Having dug all the vacant ground, wait for a day when the top is frozen and then lime the area destined to grow brassicas next season.

Winter digging to the full depth of the spade.

35

15. COMMON PESTS AND DISEASES

The best protection against pests and diseases is to grow plants well and practice good husbandry, for only strong, healthy plants will produce the best results. If, despite this, a pest or disease problem should arise, it may be necessary to resort to chemical control. There are several important points to remember:

1. Read the directions carefully before opening the container.
2. Make sure that the product is recommended for the problem on the crop you intend to spray or dust.
3. Diluted liquid insecticides and fungicides deteriorate fairly quickly, so it is advisable not to mix larger quantities than are required for immediate use.
4. Always store garden chemicals out of reach of children keep them in their original containers, making sure that the labels are always readable.

The chemicals recommended here are safe to use and free from residue risks in the vegetables provided they are used according to the makers' directions.

Remember, too, that all diseased material must be burned immediately, never composted or left lying about.

PESTS	DAMAGE	PLANTS	TREATMENT
Aphids (Greenfly, etc.)	Suck sap from leaves, causing distortion and loss of vigour. They also spread virus diseases.	Lettuce, peas, beans, etc. Practically all vegetables.	Spray with Malathion and repeat when necessary, always in the evening when bees are inactive.
Cabbage aphid (Grey Aphid)	Cripples leaves and shoots.	All brassicas, especially brussels sprouts.	Spray 'Long Last' insecticide (PBI), adding a little washing-up liquid to make foliage wetter.
Cabbage Root Fly (Cabbage Root Maggot)	The white maggots feed on the roots and so kill the plant.	All brassicas, especially cauliflowers.	Apply Bromophos granules to the planting hole and follow a fortnight later with dilute HCH; or use impregnated brassica collars.

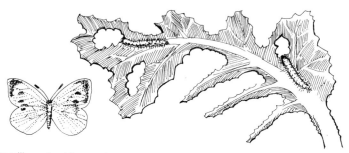

Caterpillars of cabbage white butterflies on foliage.

PESTS	DAMAGE	PLANTS	TREATMENT
Cabbage White Butterfly	The caterpillars eat the leaves.	All brassicas, especially cabbages.	Spray with a Derris insecticide as soon as the butterflies appear.
Carrot Fly	The larvae attack the roots, checking growth and making the carrots unusable.	Carrots; parsley is also subject to attack.	Apply Bromophos to open seed drill, follow up by watering seedlings with dilute HCH.
Celery Fly (Leaf Miner)	The larvae feeding on the leaves cause large blisters and trails, which check growth.	Celery and celeriac.	Spray with HCH or Fenetrothion in June.
Lettuce Root Aphid	Feeds on the roots, causing yellowing, stunting and death of the plant. Critical months June and July, especially if there are Lombardy Poplars nearby (overwintering host).	Lettuce.	Thoroughly water affected young plants with dilute Malathion.
Onion Fly	The maggot eats the roots, especially of direct-sown onions	Onions and related crops.	Apply Bromophos granules to open seed drill, follow up by watering seedlings with dilute HCH.
Pea Moth	The maggots feed on the peas in the pods. A problem on crops that flower June-August.	Peas.	Spray with Fenetrothion in the evening when flowering starts, repeat a fortnight later.

Pests/Diseases	Damage	Plants	Treatment
Potato-Cyst Eelworm	Infested plants die off early and fail to crop.	Potatoes.	Always wash seed potatoes to remove any cysts. Maintain strict crop rotation. Apply compost or other organic matter liberally to the soil. Never plant on infested ground.
Blackfly	Sucks the sap from stems and leaves.	Broad beans.	Spray with PBI 'Long Last' before the pods start growing. Alternatively, pinch out the young growing tips.
Red Spider Mite	Sucks leaf sap, causing serious damage to the plants generally.	Cucumbers and tomatoes, especially in the greenhouse.	Spray with Dimethoate, maintain relatively high humidity by watering the centre path at midday; clean the greenhouse thoroughly during the winter.
Slugs and snails	Chewed foliage.	Most young plants.	Place slug pellets or baits under cover of a box with the bottom slat removed as a safeguard for pets. Slug-tape round plants or plot is also effective.
Whitefly	Feed on the foliage, secreting a sticky honey-dew which encourages moulds. Troublesome on brassicas in areas where the crops are in continuous production.	Tomatoes, especially in the greenhouse.	Suspend 'Aeroxon Flying Insect Traps' above the plants or spray with PBI 'Long Last' insecticide twice a week. Difficult to control on brassicas; may need a winter without the host plants to break the cycle.
Botrytis (Grey Mould)	Attacks leaves and stems.	Greenhouse tomatoes, cucumbers, etc., overwintering lettuce.	Raise the greenhouse temperature, ventilate well, never overheat water. Remove all infected material, clear away all debris.

Celery Leafspot (Celery Blight)	Black disease spots quickly spread in cool damp weather.	Celery and celeriac.	Seed is usually treated against this disease. At first sign spray with a liquid copper fungicide.
Clubroot	Swollen roots, plants wilt and die; the disease can live in the soil for many years.	All brassicas. If your garden is free of this disease, always grow your own plants.	Apply Armillatox as directed for clubroot each season. Garden lime discourages the disease but *nothing* completely eliminates it from the soil.
Damping-off Disease	Seedlings collapse and die after germination in an infected compost.	Seedlings raised indoors, especially tomatoes.	Use sterilised compost, water seedlings with Cheshunt Compound solution at first signs.

Blackfly infesting broad bean.

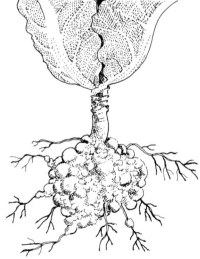

Clubroot on brassica plant.

DISEASES	DAMAGE	PLANTS	TREATMENT
Leaf Mould	Grey patches on undersides of leaves which turn brown, like thick felt.	Greenhouse tomatoes.	Increase ventilation, remove lower foliage to improve air circulation. Spray with Carbendazine (Super Carb or Boots Systemic Fungicide).
Powdery Mildew	White mildew patches on the leaves, eventually killing the plant.	Greenhouse cucumbers.	Spray with Carbendazine (Super-Carb or Boots Systemic Fungicide). Keep area around the greenhouse weed free.
Wilt Disease	Plants collapse and die.	Greenhouse tomatoes and cucumbers grown in the greenhouse border.	Switch over to peat growing bags or replace greenhouse soil before replanting.
Virus Diseases	Spread by greenfly, etc. Foliage is mottled, distorted and curled.	Potatoes, lettuce, tomatoes, cucumbers, etc.	Maintain strict control of all sucking insects with Malathion or PBI 'Long-Last', etc.
Potato Blight	Tops are dis-coloured and die within 48 hours.	Potatoes.	At first sign cut off all the tops to prevent the disease reaching the tubers. Leave tubers for another 14 days before lifting.

16. CATALOGUE OF VEGETABLES

ARTICHOKES

Globe artichokes

Very popular on the continent but regarded here as a luxury vegetable and not often found growing in small home gardens. Since the only edible parts of the artichoke are the fleshy scales enclosing the unopened flower head, the quantity of edible crop in relation to growing space is low. Best results are obtained on the lighter, warmer and well drained soils, in an open, sunny position. Dig the ground well before planting, incorporating plenty of well-rotted compost or manure.

Growing from seed is not recommended because of variation that occurs in seedlings. Start with rooted plants or propagate from established plants by taking suckers in March or April, removing them cleanly with a sharp knife from close to the main stem, with some growing root attached. Pot the suckers singly in 5 in pots in a peat-based compost; when well rooted, plant them out in rows 40 in apart, with a space of 2 ft between each plant.

In the first season there will be only one or two heads per plant, but this will eventually increase to five or six per plant. After five years' cropping, the number and size of heads decrease, so take and root fresh suckers as replacements. The heads mature between July and October and should be cut before they open. In dry weather water well to keep the plant going strongly.

At the end of the season cut the plants down. Although they are winter hardy, a light covering of straw or bracken over the crowns is a useful insurance.

'Gros Vert de Laon' is an excellent variety with first-class flavour.

Jerusalem artichokes

Useful as a screen plant, with steams 6-8 ft tall, but worth cultivating for its pleasant chestnut flavour when cooked, and a good base for soup. The crop is not fussy about soil or semi-shade, and needs no fertilisers, although a little compost before planting will help to produce larger tubers. The tubers dry out quickly, so once lifted cover them with some soil or damp sacking. They can be left in the ground during the water, lifted as necessary. Dig the remainder in February or March and re-plant the smaller tubers 3 in deep and about 8 in apart. In October the hard stems should be cut down to ground level and burned.

ASPARAGUS

Although a luxury vegetable, there is no reason why the home gardener should not allocate the limited space required for at least a single row. It is, in fact, an extremely easy crop to grow, provided you start with clean land and have the patience to wait three years after planting before cutting the first spears. Once established, the maintenance of an asparagus bed in first-class condition depends on a simple routine throughout each season.

If you start from seed, April is the best time to sow, in a clean seed-bed. To ensure good germination the seed drill should be shallow, ½ in deep; and for really strong seedlings sow the seed thinly. Each seedling will need 6 in within the row; if they come up more closely, some thinning out will be needed. By the following April the one-year-old crowns can be transplanted into their permanent growing and cropping situation; alternatively, the crowns can stay put for a second season, and if the female seed-bearing plants can be identified, these should be discarded before the final planting. In a permanent bed of all-male plants the yield of spears is greater and there is no continuous job of weeding out the seedlings.

For starting with crowns, again the time to plant is April. Whilst two- or three-year-old crowns are available, one-year olds transplant better and are cheaper. In any event, you have to wait until the third year after planting before starting to cut for the kitchen. In the case of asparagus, double digging pays off, especially when some well-rotted compost or manure is incorporated below. The ground must be completely clean of perennial weeds. Apply a top dressing of

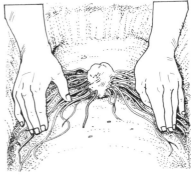

Asparagus roots should be spread out over a ridge at the bottom of the trench.

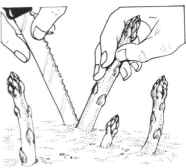

Asparagus spears should be cut just above the crown.

garden lime in March. Order crowns for mid-April delivery. Avoid the roots getting dry and cover them with damp sacking whilst planting. To plant, dig a trench 10 in deep and 12 in wide, make a sloping ridge in the bottom so that the crowns sit on it with their roots sloping downwards, and cover carefully with fine soil. For a three-row bed allow 18 in between the rows and 16 in between the crowns.

Heavy cropping and the health of the plants depend on the extensive root build-up which takes two complete growing seasons. Hand weeding incurs no risk or damage to spearbuds just below the surface. The cutting season begins when the first spearbuds appear and should stop by the third week of June; to continue would weaken the crowns and jeopardise the following season's crop. In October cut down the dead yellow fern and top dress the bed with compost; during the winter give the bed a dressing of garden lime.

Plant 'Regal Strain' or start with 'Connover's Colossal' seed.

BROAD BEANS

Broad beans would be far more popular if they were always gathered young, well before the skins get tough, and if the varieties grown were more carefully chosen. There are two distinct types: the long pod varieties, which if sown in the autumn will survive the winter, and the shorter podded Windsors, which have the best flavour and cooking qualities and which should not be sown until the spring. Within

Broad bean 'The Sutton'.

both groups there are white and green seeded varieties, differing little in flavour.

Overwintering

Cold soils which lie wet for long periods during the winter are really unsuitable; either the seed rots before germination or the young plants suffer loss of root activity or fall victim to fungus diseases later on. If you have a well-drained, somewhat sheltered site, the disease hazards can be overcome by a non-poisonous seed-dressing treat-

ment whilst the seed is still in the packet. The most popular variety for autumn sowing is 'Aquadulce'. Spring varieties, such as 'The Sutton', can be sown singly in peat pots in February and the plants brought on slowly in a cool greenhouse to be ready for planting out under cloches mid-March, to be enjoyed well ahead of autumn-sown crops.

Sowing and growing

Broad beans, like other legumes, appreciate well-prepared ground with good drainage and some

well-rotted compost worked into it some weeks ahead of sowing. On most soils a pre-sowing application of super phosphate of lime ensures a good flowering and a good bean set; and if the soil is acid, this can be corrected by an application of garden lime. The masses of root nodules on the plants produce nitrogen naturally, so there is no need for fertiliser.

Without protection, March is a good month to sow the dwarf variety 'The Sutton' in double rows 16 in apart, where the drills are 2 in deep and the seed spaced 8 in apart. For taller varieties, allow more space per plant, with the seed 10 in apart and 2 ft between each row. This variety is ideal where space is limited; the plants are only 18 in tall and do not need staking. For the tall varieties a few canes and lengths of string will be needed to prevent the top-heavy plants flopping over. In all cases moisture is essential for good growth and cropping, so don't forget to water during dry weather.

Broad beans, especially those sown in the autumn, will need checking from time to time for the first colony of black fly. The preliminary build-up always starts in the growing tips; with these removed promptly, further treatment is seldom necessary. Alternatively, a spray with PBI 'Long Last' in the evening, when the flowers have set, will control the pest.

DWARF AND CLIMBING FRENCH BEANS

Both are easy to grow, some newer varieties being heavier and more reliable croppers than runner beans, with the bonus of more tender flesh and better flavour.

Dwarf French beans
For a very early crop seed can be sown in a greenhouse subject to the temperature being kept at

Dwarf broad beans protected against birds by netted cloche.

around 55°F (13°C). Sow two seeds in a 5 in pot, using a peat-based compost. Soon after germination, eliminate the weaker seedling in each pot, and feed developing plants occasionally with a liquid tomato fertiliser. Alternatively, sow the seed 2 in deep in the greenhouse border, with a final spacing of the plants 8 in apart. Under glass red spider can be a problem, but a daily watering of the centre path and light overhead spraying of the plants deters the pests. For sowing outdoors, wait until the soil conditions are right, around the end of May or early June. If you have cloches and a greenhouse to raise the plants in 3 in pots, you could plant out under protection at the end of May or early June to crop about a fortnight earlier, but do remember to harden the plants off; they will not tolerate frost. French beans do best on well-prepared ground, with well-rotted compost at the time of winter digging. In spring apply garden lime and super phosphate of lime; no extra nitrogen is needed as the plants make their own.

Treat the seed before sowing with a seed dressing, a precaution which usually results in better germination and healthier plants. If magpies are around, cover the seed with netted cloches. Sow the seed 2 in deep, spaced 10 in apart in the row and 12 in between rows. Repeat sowings up to the end of June can be made for a succession of cropping throughout the growing season. The plants will need some water during hot dry spells. Blackfly, as soon as it is spotted, should be controlled with a Malathion insecticide, this is effective and safe, even if the beans are picked the following day.

'Amira' is the best variety for quality, flavour and quantity. 'Kinghorn Waxpod', with its round golden pods, is good, as also is 'Sprite'. All freeze well and do not need stringing if gathered young. For harvesting when fully ripe and drying, the heavy cropper 'Comtesse de Chambord' haricot bean is first class. The pods are shorter than ordinary dwarf beans and although they can be picked young and cooked whole their real role is for drying and use as a high protein food. Cultivation is the same as for ordinary French beans.

Climbing French beans

These are the beans grown by UK commercial growers in heated greenhouses and marketed as a luxury vegetable early in the year. On the continent, however, they are grown outside by commercial and amateur growers alike. One outstanding variety bred in Holland is 'Romore', which does not drop its flowers, crops early and heavily and no strings to strip away. The flesh is tender, the flavour superb, and it freezes extremely well. The young plants are slightly less sturdy at the start than runner beans and certainly need a first tie to the supports. If 'Romore' seed is scarce, use Marshall's 'Hunter' or Dobie's 'Kwintus'.

RUNNER BEANS

Our changeable British springs and summers are ideal for runner beans, but in abnormally dry seasons the plants may flower profusely without producing beans. Normally runner beans will crop continuously from early July onwards until the first autumn frosts cut them down. For the best cropping results, open up a trench 2 ft deep and 3 ft wide before Christmas or at the latest in January, so that there is plenty of time for the frost, wind and rain to work on the soil heaped up on each side of

Runner beans.

the trench. Having opened the trench, fork up the bottom soil to break any hard pan; this greatly improves root activity. Then put some well-rotted compost or manure in the bottom, or, as an alternative, old rags or newspapers, as an underlying moisture-holding sponge. Cover with a little soil to keep everything moist and prevent any of it being blown away while the trench is still open. Now apply garden lime and basic slag to the mounds of soil on the side (if the latter is difficult to obtain use super phosphate of lime instead). This combination prevents flower drop if the soil is acid. By March it is time to fill in the trench, thus allowing sufficient time for the soil to settle before sowing or planting in May. On poorish soils an overall application now of a general fertiliser will prevent the plants running out of steam before the end of the season.

For an early crop, sow seed in the greenhouse towards the end of April, using a peat-based compost and 3 in pots, one seed in each. Plants raised this way are ready by mid-May, when there is still a risk of frosts in many areas, so as an insurance pop a seed at the foot of each cane when planting out. Four 8 ft canes, arranged in wigwam fashion, 40 in apart at the base and tied together at the top, will support the crop and simplify picking. Space the wigwams 40 in apart. Outdoor

A fine crop of runner beans growing wigwam fashion.

sowing dates vary according to the district, but mid-May is as a rule safe. If plants are reluctant to twine around the canes, tie them with soft string early on. Keep the beans closely picked; seeding stops bean production. In the event of flower drop, water the soil round the plants with lime water (a small handful of hydrated lime in 2 gallons of water).

Varieties: 'Achievement', 'Enorma', 'Prizewinner', etc. 'Scarlet Emperor' is the best one for the table.

BEETROOT

A very popular and easy vegetable to grow. Successional sowings and winter storage will ensure a supply of tender beetroot throughout the year. Whilst light to medium soils suit beetroot best, good cropping results can be obtained on heavy clays, provided there is suitable winter digging and seed-bed preparation. As with most other root crops, the beetroot growing area should not be freshly manured; ideally beetroot should follow a crop that enjoyed a liberal manuring treatment the previous season. Before sowing, wait for the soil to warm up slightly, otherwise there is a risk of earlier sowings running to seed (bolting) before producing sizeable roots. One variety less likely to do this is 'Boltardy'. Another is the round variety 'Sutton's Globe', with far better colour and flesh qualities.

Sow the seed singly in shallow drills 1 in deep and 8 in apart. As

each one is really a cluster of seeds in a single container, seedlings should be thinned out at an early stage, so as to leave one strong seedling in each position. Seed of the younger and smaller 'Baby Beetroots', popular for summer salads, may be sown much closer together, at half the distance, with virtually no thinning out; and sowings can be repeated at six- weekly intervals until the end of June. To add an extra colour to the salad bowl sow a short row of 'Golden Beetroot'; but don't cook them together with the red ones as they will all come out red. For maincrop and winter use, 'Detroit Red Globe' is a useful and readily available variety for an early July sowing. For exhibition a well-grown plate of 'Libero', with dark flesh and no white rings, will take some beating; and a long beetroot for the same purpose is 'Cheltenham Green Top'.

For best results, grow in full sunshine; and to avoid loss of colour from 'bleeding', allow the tops to wilt for a day or so before twisting them off prior to cooking or storing. The much recommended winter storage in containers filled with sand or peat is not always satisfactory; in time they either dry out or become too damp, so that the beetroot either shrivels or goes rotten. Beetroot plants will overwinter where they have grown, given some protection with, say, dry bracken, but in gardens with heavy clay it is better to lift and store the beetroot in a small outside clamp, under a covering of straw and soil. Small beetroots are best for freezing; cooked in the usual way they store in plastic bags without any loss of quality.

BRASSICAS

BRUSSELS SPROUTS

These are the most popular of all the home-grown brassica crops. With the introduction of numerous F1 Hybrid varieties, it is now possible to start picking sprouts in July and to continue until March, although with a choice of so many other excellent summer vegetables, the season normally commences in October. One of the best varieties for Christmas is 'Troika', an F2 Hybrid, the seed of which is much cheaper than F1 Hybrid seed.

Many of the F1 Hybrid varieties have been bred and introduced for commercial growers who need sprouts that mature all together at the same time from top to bottom on the stem so as to be harvested by machine either for the fresh or frozen food markets. Amateur gardeners, who require sound, solid sprouts with

Brussels sprouts 'Pegasus'.

little waste and plenty of flavour after they are cooked, need to grow varieties with sprouts that start maturing at the bottom and slowly go on with the process to the top. Some varieties have relatively large tops which when cut at the halfway sprout-picking stage make a useful green cabbage for cooking as a separate vegetable. Removal of these tops directs more energy into the swelling of the unpicked sprouts. 'Ormavon' is one such variety and well worth growing. Other recommendable varieties are 'Peer Gynt' (F1) short stemmed and well suited to a windswept garden, and 'Pegasus', slightly taller, with tightly packed dark green sprouts full of flavour; both are October to November croppers. 'Troika' follows for December and January, and 'Aries', an outstanding frost-resistant variety, to end the season from February to March.

Only by growing from seed can you be sure of the variety and, more important, avoid the risk of introducing club root. Sow seed in mid-March in shallow seed-bed drills ½ in deep; the thinner the seed is sown, the stronger the seedling plants will be for transplanting in May or early June. Transplant in rows 3 ft apart, and try to space the same distance between the plants in the row. The ground needs to be firm, well settled after winter digging, with an application of garden lime. To prevent the cabbage root fly maggot damage, either water each plant with dilute HCH insecticide or sprinkle Bromophos granules around the base of the stems. Alternatively, when planting, place impregnated brassica collars around each stem at ground level. Later, when the plants are established, give each one a small handful of a general fertiliser and hoe it in without disturbing the roots. At the end of the season lift the bare stems without delay and burn them to reduce the risk of white fly.

CABBAGES

Spring cabbage

As the name indicates, it comes in for cutting in the spring, a time when fresh vegetables are often scarce. Most varieties are winter hardy. Sow the seed thinly, in late July or early August, in a shallow seed-bed drill; about eight weeks later sturdy plants should be ready for transplanting. Alternatively, sow the seed directly into the growing row, and thin out plants later to 8 in; then when the plants are full of leaf, cut every other one and leave the rest to heart up in April and May.

Plant in firm soil with a dibber, treading it around each plant with the heel. If the spring cabbage is to follow a previous brassica crop, an overall pre-planting or sowing application of a general fertiliser will be needed. Early in the new year a dessertspoonful of nitro-chalk or sulphate of ammonia around each plant will stimulate growth especially if lightly hoed in; the faster the plants grow, the better and more tender the cabbage. Occasional surface cultivation between the plants will control

Cabbage 'Offenham'.

the weeds and also let some air into the soil.

Of several useful varieties, the earliest to heart are 'April' or 'Harbinger'. 'Offenham' is slightly later but produces much larger hearts, and 'Wheeler's Imperial' is an early cropper with smallish but very compact hearts.

Summer cabbage

The first summer cabbage seed can be sown in the greenhouse February-March for planting out under cloches. Very little heat is required for germination, with the seedlings pricked out into 3 in pots and subsequently hardened off. Robust plants can be put out early April. 'Greyhound' and 'Hispi', a great F1 Hybrid cabbage, are both suitable.

For a main summer crop, sow seed in March-April in a prepared seed-bed. A sprinkling of Bromophos along the shallow open drill will help ward off cabbage root fly. Immediately after germination, if the weather turns hot and dry, apply Derris dust along the row to prevent flea beetle damage. Ground conditions, planting and feeding are as for spring cabbage; but now, with more pests around, it is sound practice to sprinkle Bromophos in the dibber hole before firming the plants in with the heel, watering a fortnight later with dilute HCH insecticide, a combined treatment that is most effective against the cabbage root maggot. Later in the summer, have some Derris insecticide handy, ready for the appearance of the first cabbage white butterflies.

Planting distances should be related to the size of the variety, starting at 16 in between rows and the plants in the rows, or better still, 2 ft each way. Good varieties include 'Golden Acre', 'Greyhound' and 'Winningstadt', the last being the large pointed cabbage so often seen on the show bench.

Savoys

These are winter hardy, the outer leaf foliage dark green and somewhat crinkly, and the mature hearts more loosely folded than those of ordinary cabbage. By careful choice of varieties, it is possible to start cutting as early as September and to continue until April. Preparation of the seed-bed and planting out ground is as for other brassicas. Early maturing varieties can be sown in April; for the late ones early May is better. Plants will be ready for transplanting in about eight weeks,

not longer, otherwise they become weak and straggly. Leave 2 ft between the plants and the rows. For the earliest Savoy crop try 'Best of All', and for the scarce vegetable season, February-March, 'Alexander's No. 1', which has dark green foliage, more than usually compact hearts, and good flavour. 'Late Ormskirk' is another extremely useful late season variety.

Winter cabbage

The hearts of these winter hardy cabbages are solid and tightly packed. Of the recently introduced 'January King' series, the selection 'January King Asmer Special', which can be cut from January till March, is the best of several varieties. For an earlier cut try 'Christmas Drumhead', a dwarf grower with good compact hearts full of flavour. 'Aquarius', an F1 Hybrid, is a smaller cabbage than 'January King' and can be planted a little more closely. The F1 Hybrid 'Celtic', with large, solid hearts, can be cut up to the end of January.

Dutch white cabbage

Worth considering in districts where heavy snowfalls cover the ground for long periods. Interest has developed sufficiently for seed to be listed in the amateur catalogues. Growing procedures are the same as for other winter brassicas. They can either be cut as green cabbage in the autumn, or stored out of the ground. For storage the plants should be pulled up completely with the roots (soil removed) and the outer leaves peeled off to the white hearts; these will keep in good condition for weeks in an airy frost-free shed or a well-ventilated cellar. 'Jupiter', an F1 Hybrid, makes a hard round cabbage with a white, crisp, excellently flavoured heart.

All these winter brassicas will need protecting against cabbage root fly and caterpillars during the growing season.

Red pickling cabbage

Worth its place among the brassicas, either for pickling or cooking as a fresh vegetable. Seed sown in March or early April will produce cabbages ready for cutting from early autumn onwards. Growing procedures are exactly the same as for summer cabbage. Good varieties are 'Red Drumhead' and 'Giant Blood Red'.

Calabrese

A very quick-growing green sprouting broccoli. Sown in April or early May, the tightly packed shoots (spears) can be cut in August-September, when they are deliciously tender, with a flavour not unlike asparagus. Always cut the main head shoot first, after which the side shoots come thick and fast. As with all broccolis, the more constant the cutting, the greater the production of quality shoots.

Sow and grow in the same way as other summer brassicas. Open pollinated varieties, with a lengthy cutting period, include 'Autumn Spear' and 'Italian Sprouting', both a little later than 'Express Corona', an F1 Hybrid, which could be ready during August.

White and purple sprouting broccoli

Both are much slower growing than calabrese. In fact, there will be roughly twelve months from the time the seed is sown to the end of the cropping, which can create problems in an intensively cropped vegetable garden. In severe winters, too, the plants suffer foliage damage, although they usually recover when the weather turns milder. Growing procedures are as for other brassica crops, but plant 2½ ft apart each way. Varieties: 'Purple Sprouting' very hardy, starting to produce its purple shoots in March; 'Late Purple Sprouting', equally hardy, cropping late April into May; and 'Improved White', not quite so hardy but delicious when its white shoots mature in March-April.

Kale (Borecole)

Despite, its lack of popularity, kale makes a good winter vegetable dish, with the leaf ribs removed before cooking. Treat as any other winter brassica, planting 2 ft apart each way. Start by picking the lower leaves and the plant will go on producing more and more leaves higher up the stem; in March it will grow another crop of tender young leaves on otherwise bare stems. 'Dwarf Green Curled Kale' is an attractive looking plant. 'Pentland Brig' is tougher still, the variety for the rigorous conditions in northern England and Scotland. 'Thousand Headed Kale', with its masses of white shoots all through the winter, is not quite so hardy.

Cauliflower

Cauliflowers are often regarded as difficult to grow. Any check during the growing season can easily result in 'buttoning' (mini cauliflowers); and for complete and consistent success, sowing of the variety or varieties concerned must be precisely at the right time. In the southern half of the country it is possible to crop home-grown cauliflowers for the greater part of the year, whereas farther north there are limitations.

The varieties available stem from plant-breeding work done in many countries. From northern Europe come varieties such as 'Classic', 'Snowball' and 'Dominant', dwarf and quick maturing, the type for sowing under glass to plant out in April when the soil has lost some of its winter cold. 'All the Year Round' is of French origin, probably still the best for a seed-bed sowing in April and transplanting in June, to crop in August-September. For later autumn cropping until the frost arrives, varieties of Mediterranean origin, such as 'Flora Blanca', sowing must be delayed until late May, otherwise the curds are liable to be spoiled with interleafing. So sow in May, and transplant or thin out in the row in late June or early July. For a March-April crop, sow a Dutch variety with extra winter hardiness. 'Armado-April' and 'Thanet' mature in April whilst 'Birchington' and 'Armado-May' come roughly a month later.

Soil conditions are extremely important, with a high level of fertility essential. Plant on an area that has been well prepared with compost or manure dug in some months before, so that the ground has had time to settle down; planting on loose soil is fatal. An overall application of a general fertiliser before planting is always beneficial, reducing the risk of a plant check. Water to prevent dryness at the roots. Cabbage root fly adores cauliflowers, so apply Bromophos in the seed drill and in the planting out holes, and follow this up by watering the plants with a dilute HCH insecticide a fortnight later. Direct sowing in the row reduces the risk but the plants should still be watered with this insecticide after thinning out. Prevent yellowing of the curds by folding the nearest large leaves over them.

CARROTS

A popular vegetable that can be presented to the table fresh from the garden at almost any time of the year. It is an easy subject to grow out of season in an unheated greenhouse border or a cold frame. Outdoors, under the protection of cloches, young succulent carrots are a treat to enjoy in June. Without any protection it is necessary to wait until April before making the first sowing; then you should be pulling carrots in July. Sow at monthly intervals for a succession of tender, tasty carrots throughout the summer months, and towards the end of June or

Folding a leaf over a cauliflower curd.

early July for the larger main crop carrots for autumn and winter use.

Carrots do best in light to medium-type soils, but can be grown successfully on much heavier and even clay soils, provided the pre-sowing preparation of the seed-bed is done well. In a cold greenhouse or cold frame it is just a question of lightening and improving the growing medium by working in materials such as granulated peat, washed sand or ashes. Outside it is best to start preparing the ground well before Christmas. Start by digging it deeply to the full depth of a new spade and leaving it roughly dug so that the winter frosts can freeze the water held in the clay and separate the clay particles. By the end of March, the top soil will be ready for

breaking down with a cultivator into an acceptable carrot-growing medium. On no account re-dig the winter dug ground in the spring before preparing for seed sowing; and never sow on freshly manured or compost treated land if you wish to have perfectly shaped straight carrots rather than fork-rooted specimens. 'Growmore' fertiliser at the rate of 2 oz to the square yard, raked in before sowing, is safer and better.

Because carrot seed is very small, the seed-drill must always be extremely shallow, so that the seed will only be just covered with fine soil. Sow as thinly as possible to avoid unnecessary thinning out of the seedlings, an activity which encourages the carrot fly to lay its eggs on the remaining plants. To combat this pest, sprinkle Bromophos along the open seed-drill and water later on, when the seedlings are established, with dilute HCH insecticide. Allow at least 1 ft between rows and prevent weed competition by regular use of the hoe.

For the first sowing in an unheated greenhouse or cold frame February is a good time; try either 'Early Scarlet Horn' or 'Amstel' (Amsterdam Forcing). Outside in April 'Sutton's Favourite' is a superb carrot with bright, tender flesh, out-standing flavour and no hard centre core. For successional sowings 'Sutton's Favourite' is again the choice, but for the main crop, sown in July, 'Autumn King' is ideal, both for its quality on the table and its ability to withstand considerable amounts of frost when left in the ground for overwinter storage.

CELERY AND CELERIAC

Celery

Traditionally grown celery, culti-vated in a prepared trench, can still provide the crispest and sweetest heads of the best quality celery, far superior to those produced by any of the so-called 'self-blanching' varieties. Sow the seed during the last fortnight of March in half pots, germi-nating it in a propagator or on the windowsill; the ideal tempera-ture is 60°F (15°C). As soon as the seedlings are large enough to handle, prick them out in a seed-tray to grow on in good light without being allowed to dry out. In May they are hardened off for planting out in June.

In early spring, prepare a trench 18 in wide and 12 in deep, with a goodly covering of well-rotted compost worked into the bottom. The plants, still in trays, can be 'hardened off' outdoors, in a sheltered spot, for a week or so. Then they should be planted with a trowel in the bottom of the trench about 10 in apart, with as little root disturbance as poss-ible. From then until full growth, keep them well watered, remembering that they are bog plants by nature.

When the plants are fully grown, start earthing up – a

Carrots 'Early Nantes'.

59

process that blanches the stems – giving each one a light tie with soft string or raffia to keep the soil out of the heads. Begin carefully with a trowel and afterwards with a spade, doing the job in staggered stages over a period of several weeks. The plants will eventually be growing in a mound of soil 10-12 in higher than the garden level. Suitable varieties are 'Solid White', for early use, and later on either 'Giant Pink' or 'Giant Red'.

Celery 'Giant Pink'.

Self blanching celery is grown in an identical manner, but the procedure is less complicated as it is only necessary to winter dig the ground, incorporating at the same time some well-rotted compost. Planting begins in June, and complete blanching of the stems is achieved by close planting in a block instead of separate rows. A square block is best, with the plants 8 in apart each way; a few lathes of light wood fixed close to the outer plants will ensure that they, too, blanch properly. During the growing season an occasional liquid feed and watering whenever the weather is dry will be appreciated. Varieties include 'Celebrity', 'Lathom Self Blanching', 'Jason Self Blanching', 'Golden Self Blanching' and 'American Green'. None of these are frost hardy.

Celeriac

A stump-rooted celery, even better for soup making and for use in stews, etc., than the stick celery. The roots are not frost hardy and should be lifted for use during the winter. Plant growing and raising are as for celery except that it is best to allow 12 in between the plants in the row. No trench is necessary. Avoid a growing check after planting out, which results in smaller bulbous roots rather than large ones. In the autumn draw some soil up over the roots, and lift for storage in December. For long-term storage use a clamp, but for shorter periods a frost-free airy shed will be sufficient protection.

CUCUMBERS

For the home gardener the use of a heated greenhouse for cropping cucumbers early in the season is a non-starter on account of the cost of maintaining the required temperature. But wait until the end of April, then plant the right variety in an unheated greenhouse and success can be yours. Nowadays there are varieties that only produce female flowers, so that the daily task of removing male flowers is eliminated. 'Renova' and 'Athene' are recommendable not only on account of their long fruits, excellent flavour and great salad qualities, but also their cropping ability when grown without heat. For a more abundant crop of half-length cucumbers, try 'Petita'; cut when 10 in long, the quality is superb.

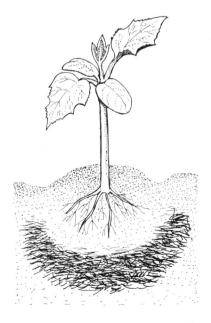

Planting a ridge cucumber.

61

For end of April planting, sow the seeds in mid-March, singly on edge in 3 in pots, using a peat-based seed compost; then after watering, some warmth will be required for germination – 65°F (18°C) is ideal. This can be achieved in a propagating frame or even on a windowsill over the radiator in the daytime, moving the pots to the centre of the room at night. The seedlings will grow rapidly indoors, always in a place where the light is good and the air not too dry.

Growing in a prepared mound of stacked turf or cooled strawy horse manure gives good results, but a practical alternative is PBI growing 'Bolsters', each to contain two plants, placed in line lengthwise about 12 in from the side of the greenhouse. Loosely

Stop cucumber laterals after formation of third leaf.

tie the fast-growing main stems with raffia to the lowest wire. Old varieties such as 'Improved Telegraph' are cropped on the laterals (side shoots); with 'Renova', 'Athene' and 'Petita', all the laterals are pinched out, with cropping on the main stems. Tying for support continues until the main stem reaches the ridge of the greenhouse, when it can either be carried over and down the other side or the growing tip pinched out.

Cucumbers appreciate warmth with humidity and some shading from fierce sunlight. A regular midday watering of the centre path prevents red spider becoming a serious pest problem. Avoid, if possible, overhead spraying, which often induces the onset of mildew; if it does become necessary for the control of red spider, leave the door open during the day. Feed with a liquid tomato fertiliser about a month after planting out, with repeat applications at fortnightly intervals. Do not feed with inorganic fertilisers such as sulphate of ammonia, as this frequently causes bitterness. At all times watering is important; drying out of the growing medium causes wilting, followed by cucumbers going soft with rot at the blossom end. From mid-June onwards shade the greenhouse on the sunny side, spraying or brushing on 'Coolglass'.

In an unheated frame the growing technique is basically the same, except that the plants are grown lying down, so the length of stems for cropping is limited to the size of the frame. Place two plants in each

'Bolster', placed lengthwise at the high end of the frame. Give some shading to avoid scorching, and ventilate on summer days by slightly raising the lights. Watering the soil underneath the foliage creates a good humidity level. Feeding is as for plants in the greenhouse.

Ridge cucumbers are the varieties bred for growing outdoors. Sow in April, germinating the seed as for indoor cucumbers, and grow them on indoors until safe to plant out when the danger of night frosts has passed, perhaps keeping under cloches for about a week. Plant about 3 ft apart into a pocket of well-rotted compost, leaving a shallow depression around each plant for easy watering. Treatment during the growing season is the same as for indoor cucumbers. The varieties 'Burpless Tasty Green' and 'Long Green' will both do well, especially in warmer areas.

Gherkins

Grown in the same way as cucumbers, these can be fruited on the main stem as well as on the laterals. The plants are quite vigorous and will take up a fair amount of space in the greenhouse. The fruit is picked when about the size of a finger and used for pickling. Variety 'Venlo Pickling'.

LEEKS

Although they can be grown for early lifting in the autumn, it is during the winter months when leeks are generally appreciated. The winter hardy varieties survive unharmed in perfect condition for the kitchen once the thaw sets in.

Like all members of the onion family, they do best in fertile soil well supplied with plant nutrients. Start preparations well before Christmas, by winter digging the area and incorporating well-rotted compost. To ensure continuity of growth throughout the season, work in some organically based fertiliser, either fish, blood and bone or PBI 'Back to Nature' fertiliser, when breaking down the remains of the winter-dug clods. Give at least two top dressings of the same fertiliser in the summer or early autumn.

Plant in an open, sunny position. Leeks never do well in the shade, especially if the soil is also dry. Water thoroughly in the evening and make sure that the water gets down to the roots. Seed for early leeks can be sown in the greenhouse early March, using a peat-based seed compost in a 5 in half pot. When the seedlings are large enough to handle, prick them out, 28 to a standard-size seed tray, this time using a peat-based potting compost. These greenhouse raised plants should be finally hardened off outside and planted out in early May.

For the later main crop leeks, sow the seed outside in a well prepared seed-bed, making sure that any soil lumps are broken down to a fine tilth. The drill should be no more than ½ in deep, and the seed sown very thinly; overcrowding results in very weak plants, slow initial growth and often bolting to seed after planting out.

By June they should be ready for planting out. Lift them carefully with a fork, trim back any long straggly roots and, if the leaves are very long, clip a little off the ends. Use a dibber to

Leek 'Musselburgh'.

make 5 in deep holes, 6 in apart in the row, dropping a plant in each hole. With a finger over the watering can spout, dribble water down the side of the hole, which washes sufficient soil down to cover the roots. Subsequent watering or rain will fill the holes completely with soil. When growing more than one row allow at least 15 in between rows. As the leeks continue to grow, draw up the soil around the plants in order to start the blanching process.

'Musselburgh' and 'Lyon Prizetaker' are both well-known and reliable varieties, but even better are 'Giant Winter-Catalina' and 'Giant Winter-Wila'.

LETTUCE

Whatever the size of your vegetable plot, space should be allowed for lettuces; and if you own a greenhouse or cold frame, provided the varieties are chosen accordingly, you can enjoy crisp home-grown lettuce for at least eight months of the year.

For outdoor lettuce growing choose an open site, as shade produces weak leaf growth with little or no heart development. The ground should be well cultivated, with good moisture holding capacity, but avoid adding either manure or compost during the pre-sowing or planting preparations. Ideally the well-rotted compost or manure should have been applied for some other crop, twelve months ahead of the ground being used for lettuce; then you can be sure of a good crop with solid hearts.

For early outdoor lettuce, such as 'Fortune', sow seed in February in the greenhouse, setting the propagator to a temperature of 61°F (17°C). Prick the seedlings out into small pots, and plant out towards the end of March under cloches. An early crop can also be obtained by sowing seed direct under cloches with the protected soil slightly warmer by mid-March.

Sowing without any protection can also start in late March provided soil conditions are good. The seed-bed tilth should be fine, dry on top with some moisture underneath. Draw out a shallow drill no more than ½ in deep with the corner of the rakehead, sow thinly, just covering seed with fine soil, and thin out the seedlings as soon as possible to 9 in apart.

When April arrives you can plan for crisp-hearted lettuces throughout the summer, sowing fortnightly in short rows. Cos lettuces prefer a soil which is beginning to warm up, provided it is still moist underneath. 'Little Gem' is an ideal space saver for the small garden needing no more than 6 in in the row after thinning out. It will

Lettuce 'Late Nyah'.

stand for weeks in good condition without bolting to seed, remaining crisp and sweet for a long time. 'Continuity' is another small lettuce with bronze-tipped leaves and tight, crisp hearts. And although the original 'Webb's Wonderful' is no longer available, 'Lake Nyah' is one of several worthy successors.

For the autumn 'Winter Density' can be sown in July, with a repeat sowing in October to stand the winter with some cloche protection; they will be ready for cutting in March or April. To keep the cold frame in use throughout the winter, prepare the soil well, sow 'Arctic King' in October, thin out early, don't water and keep the frame ventilated.

Varieties

'Fortune' for early sowings.

'Little Gem', small cos-lettuce of great quality very suitable for the small family.

'Continuity', small cabbage lettuce with very crisp heart.

'Lake Nyah', large summer lettuce with very crisp heart.

'Winter Density', cos-lettuce for late sowings.

'Arctic King', for over-wintering in a cold frame, greenhouse or under cloches.

Marrows, Courgettes, Pumpkins and Squashes

All are members of the cucumber family and consequently extremely frost sensitive, a fact which determines the growing techniques from seed sowing to the timing of outdoor plantings. Marrows have long been known here as a summer vegetable, but the French-introduced courgettes, which are simply baby marrows cut and cooked while still very young and tender, are now even more popular. Pumpkins have always been associated with Halloween, and it is the Americans who have educated us to appreciate pumpkin pie, made with small, young and tender fruits. As for squashes, their use here for the table is also derived from the continent, and nowadays the seed of numerous varieties is available.

At the seed sowing stage, all these vegetables can be treated alike, started off in the greenhouse with a view to having the plants ready for planting out towards the end of May or beginning of June. For germination the seeds require a temperature of 60°F (16°C) in a propagating frame. Sow the seeds singly in 3 in pots, using a peat-based compost and covering each seed with about 1 in of the compost.

Sow in mid-April, but allow bench space as the seedlings are large and the plants grow very quickly. Transfer plants at the beginning of May to a cold frame for hardening off. Plant out at end of May or the beginning of June, ideally providing them with cloches for at least a fortnight.

Well-rotted compost is the best growing medium for these plants. Put liberal quantities well down under each plant, where it acts as a moisture-holding sponge and a supplier of natural nutrients. Each plant is established in a saucer-like depression, making the all-important early watering more efficient. During the growing season the plants will need watering and an occasional feed with a liquid fertiliser. For a regular supply of courgettes, keep the cutting up to date as the plant tends to stop flower production if the courgettes become marrow size.

Varieties
Marrows: 'Tender and True', medium-sized, of great quality. 'Green Bush', a very free cropper.
Courgettes: 'Early Gem' (F1), dark green and very tender. 'Gold Rush', bright yellow, extremely prolific and of great quality.
Pumpkins: 'Hundredweight' or 'Mammoth Orange', excellent when cut young and will grow if left to a large size for Hallowe'en.

Marrow 'Green Bush'.

ONIONS

Most vegetable gardeners get great satisfaction from growing a successful onion crop, whether it be from sets, direct sown seed or (for the really big onions) from transplants. No outdoor vegetable crop is more responsive to good treatment; the higher the soil fertility, the better the onions, so many gardeners continue growing onions year after year on the same piece of ground. Even the dreaded disease of onion white rot can be avoided by treating the ground with Armillatox immediately after lifting the crop.

Soil preparations start each autumn with deep rough digging together with the incorporation of liberal amounts of well-rotted compost. In March, with drying winds, break down the winter-dug ground with a cultivator.

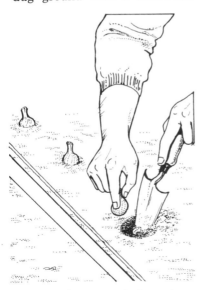

Planting onion sets against a garden line.

Give the bed a generous overall application of PBI, 'Back to Nature' or 'Growmore' fertiliser – no less than 2-4 oz per square yard (100-125 g per m²). Onions will not tolerate weed competition, so it is most important to start on clean ground and eliminate, if possible, every scrap of perennial weed roots.

Growing from onion sets
Specially prepared onion sets make growing a crop relatively easy, especially as the risk of onion fly damage is almost nil. When bought, they should be absolutely without a trace of stem growth, then kept in this condition in a dry, cool, frost-free place. Mid-April is soon enough to start planting; earlier plantings often bolt to seed. Plant the sets 9 in apart in the row, using a trowel; the tip of the set should just show above ground.

Varieties
'Rocardo', 'Marshall's Autumn Gold', 'Giant Fen Globe' and 'Stuttgart'. For exhibition try 'Marshall's Showmaster' or 'Super Ailsa Craig'.

Direct sown onions
A well prepared seed-bed with the fertiliser worked in is essential for late March-early April sowing. The seed drills need to be shallow, never more than ½ in deep and at least 1 ft between the rows. Ensure that the seed is distributed evenly along the open drill. Before raking along the drill to cover the seed, sprinkle Bromophos granules along it to deter the onion fly from laying its

eggs. Later, when the seedlings have straightened out of the loop stage, water along the row with a dilute solution of HCH.

Varieties
'Rijnsburger Robusta' and 'Rijnsburger Balstora', excellent varieties for long storage. 'Bedfordshire Champion', an old favourite, still good for keeping.

Transplanted onions
For the large onions sow the seed late December-early January in a propagator with a controlled temperature of 60°F (16°C). Germination takes about 14 days. Prick out the seedlings into seed trays or, better still, into individual 3 in pots, keeping them at a temperature not lower than 50°F (10°). After hardening off, plant

Onion 'Rijnburger', end of season.

outside mid-April. To harvest, allow the tops to die down naturally, then lift on a dry day and complete the drying process, preferably outside, but if damp under cover.

Varieties:
'Improved Mammoth', 'Red Mammoth', 'Kelsae', 'Lancastrian'.

Japanese Onions
Mild-flavoured Japanese onions are a totally new concept of onion growing from seed sown outside in August and harvested fully ripe in June or early July. Start by digging in a liberal amount of well-rotted compost and, unlike the winter digging procedure, break the top down immediately with a three-pronged cultivator to prevent excessive loss of soil moisture. Rake in some PBI 'Back to Nature' fertiliser especially good for all onions, or give the area an overall application of 'Growmore' fertiliser at the rate of 2 oz per square yard (60 g per m^2). Sow the seed thinly and evenly in a drill ½ in deep and sprinkle with Bromophos granules.

Having covered the drill with fine soil, all that needs to be done is hand weeding. At the end of February, provided the ground is not frozen, apply the same fertiliser feed between the rows to boost growth. Continue keeping the bed free of weeds. Harvesting is virtually without problems. The tops die down naturally in the summer heat, and the onions can then be lifted on a dry day for storing in the usual way. They will keep in excellent condition, without rots or breaking into growth, until about Christmas.

Varieties:
'Imai Early Yellow', 'Extra Early Kaizuka' and 'Senshyu Semi-Globe Yellow'.

Spring onions
Sow a short row of 'White Lisbon' in March, with repeat sowings if need be until August, for pulling green from June until the first frosts. For the earliest New Year salad onion sow 'White Lisbon Winter Hardy' in September, for pulling green in early spring; both are mild-flavoured. Ground and seed drill preparation, etc., are as for other onions, except that the seed can be more liberally distributed along the drill.

Shallots
This member of the onion family is excellent for pickling. Start by planting the bulbs with a trowel as soon as possible after the shortest day, then they will ripen and be ready for lifting soon after the longest day. All cultivations are as for onions.

Varieties:
'Dutch Yellow', 'Giant Red' and 'Hative de Niort', the classic exhibition shallot.

PEAS

Only those who grow their own peas and carefully select the varieties know how delicious freshly picked garden peas can be. Yet there is a tremendous difference between the table qualities of the round seeded and wrinkled seeded varieties. Although the former can be sown either in the autumn or early spring, when the ground is too cold and wet for any of the wrinkled seeded varieties, they are full of starch and have a low sugar content, whereas the reverse is true for wrinkled seeded peas.

The problem of wrinkled pea seed rotting rather than germinating when the soil is both wet and cold can be overcome by sowing 'Little Marvel' seed, early March, in small peat pots in the greenhouse, two seeds to a pot. With little or no heat needed for germination, about a month later they are ready to go outside under cloches. They can then be enjoyed as early as round seeded varieties, such as 'Feltham First', sown directly outside.

Garden peas can be grown successfully on most types of soil, provided the drainage is good. As with most vegetables, they respond best when the

Pea 'Little Marvel'.

ground has been fully prepared, especially if some well-rotted compost has been incorporated a year or so before.

For fresh garden peas throughout the summer and even early autumn, make successional sowings at about fortnightly intervals, with the latest sowing around mid-July. If you leave it any later, mildew becomes an increasing problem, and pods fail to swell. Sow in a drill of a spade width and 2 in deep, spacing the seed singly 2 in apart. After covering the seed, settle the top by a slight firming with the rake head. Use a few short sticks or canes and a length of string to keep the haulms of dwarf varieties off the ground; for taller varieties pea sticks or a length of special plastic pea netting are needed. To prevent maggots (pea moth larvae) in the pods, spray with HCH or Derris insecticide a week after flowering starts, and repeat the treatment ten days later.

Wrinkled seeded varieties

(for sowing March onwards):
'Early onward': heavy cropper, excellent quality, freezes well, height 2 ft.
'Onward': maincrop, heavy cropper, excellent quality, freezes well, height 2 ft.
'Kelvedon Wonder': resistance to mildew makes it one of the best for July sowings, height 18 in.
'Little Marvel': excellent quality, freezes well, height 18 in.
'Senator': a real winner for flavour and cropping, one of the best for freezing, height 3 ft.

Round seeded varieties

(for sowing autumn or early spring):
'Feltham First': height 18 in.
'Pilot': height 3½ ft.

PEPPERS AND AUBERGINES

Sweet peppers

Although peppers, because of their tenderness, are usually cultivated in a greenhouse, they can be grown successfully, albeit less prolifically, outside, provided the best varieties are selected. Nevertheless, a greenhouse or propagating frame capable of maintaining a temperature of 60°-65°F (16°-18°C) is required for satisfactory germination.

For an outside crop, sow seed in mid-March and prick out the seedlings into 3 in pots, using a peat-based compost. Some warmth will be needed to keep them growing without a check until they are well rooted. From then on growth both above and below compost level is rapid; a further move into 5 in pots ensures sturdier plants for transplanting outdoors. Make sure that the roots are kept moist, and avoid crowding the plants too close together on the bench or shelf. Good light is essential, so never place the plants too far away from the glass. If a greenhouse is not available, these stages can be carried out indoors on a windowsill; but if the light comes from one side only, turn the growing plants daily to prevent them bending to one side.

For planting outside choose a

Red peppers.

sunny, sheltered position and do not plant until early June when all risks of night frosts have ended. Allow 18 in between the plants and provide each one with a support cane. From then on the plants always need water, either natural or artificial, to increase the foliage cover. A fortnightly liquid tomato fertiliser feed increases their cropping ability. At first the peppers are green, the stage at which one can start picking for salads; if left for another 2-3 weeks to fully mature on the plants, they will turn red. For growing under cloches, use the larger barn types; even so, it is advisable to plant in a shallow trench or the headroom will be insufficient by cropping time.

For growing an earlier crop from start to finish in a greenhouse, use 8-10 in pots filled with a peat based compost, or growing bags. Such plants need a weekly feed with a tomato fertiliser. Support with a small cane. Both in the greenhouse and outdoors watch out for greenfly, whitefly and red spider mite, the last a really difficult pest in the greenhouse. Prevention is by regularly spraying in the early stages with PBI 'Longlast' every three weeks, and when cropping time starts with liquid Derris. Daily overhead spraying with clear water and maintaining a reasonable humid atmosphere in the greenhouse will keep red spider mite at bay.

Varieties
'New Ace' (F1 Hybrid), early yielding, suitable for both outdoors and under glass culture, good cropper, height 18-24 in.
'Bell Boy' (F1 Hybrid), also very good either outside or in the greenhouse, height 18-24 in.
'Triton' makes a compact plant and has cone-shaped fine-flavoured fruits changing from yellow to orange; a suitable variety for containers on balcony and patio, 10-12 in.

Aubergines
Generally known as eggplants on account of the shape of the young fruits, they too need warmth for germination and all subsequent stages of growth. With the introduction of new F1 Hybrid varieties, a small crop can be grown outside in a sunny, sheltered position. The procedure is the same as for peppers, sowing mid-March for outdoor cultivation or a month earlier for growing in the greenhouse. Feeding, spraying and daily care are as for peppers, including support with a small cane.

Varieties
'Moneymaker' (F1 Hybrid), produces beautiful 10 in long, dark purple fruits.
'Black Prince' (F1 Hybrid), dark purple fruits 8 in long, worth trying against a sunny wall.
'Easter Egg', a very prolific producer of white egg-shaped fruits of good flavour, suitable for the patio or in pots.

POTATOES

Certainly the best crop either for cleaning newly broken ground or

Planting potatoes.

neglected weed-ridden areas. Make sure, however, that you start with ground free from potato eelworm. Never grow potatoes more than once every three years in the same place, remove any self-set potato plants early in the season during the rotational non-potato cropping year, and be as liberal as possible with well-rotted compost when preparing the ground. In addition, wash your seed potatoes in clean water before setting them up for sprouting or planting direct from the bag.

For the gardener with limited space, it is best to concentrate on first early varieties, but with more room and careful selection of varieties, top-quality potatoes can be enjoyed all year round. Potatoes do best on medium-type soils with a good humus content. On very light soils the addition of organic manures and some watering in dry weather periods is essential. Very wet and heavy soils, even when well worked, can have autumn harvesting problems, with the risk of slug damage to maincrop varieties.

Planting

Sprouted tubers are best, especially for the earliest crop. Set the seed up in trays, eyes upwards, in a light, cool but frost-free place, as under the greenhouse bench. The growing site should be free from shade. Plant in March-April, depending on risk of late frosts. On freshly broken ground plant with a spade, digging a 5 in hole for each tuber; on well-cultivated ground open

up a trench 6 in deep to the width of a spade. Put some well-rotted compost in the bottom and for a heavier yield apply 'Growmore' fertiliser along the open trench. Use a garden line to keep the row straight. For first earlies allow 2 ft 4 in between the rows and 12 in between the tubers; for all other varieties 2½ ft between the rows and 15 in between the tubers. To economise, cut the sprouted tubers lengthwise immediately before planting and dust the cut ends with garden lime.

Potato foliage is frost sensitive, so draw fine soil over the tops whenever frost is forecast. Alternatively, if the tops are too big, cover them with several layers of newspaper. Earthing up will prevent the swelling potatoes getting exposed to the light and going green. First earlies planted in March are usually ready for lifting in July, but by using cloches until the haulms outgrow them it is possible to lift new potatoes in June.

Harvesting and storing maincrop vegetables

When the haulms have started to die down, pick a dry day to dig the crop so that the lifted potatoes can stay out on top for a few hours to dry off. An earth and straw clamp outside is best for storing a quantity, but a wooden box or hessian sack in a dry, dark, frost-free place will suffice for a small amount. Never use polythene bags or plastic boxes, as these cause sweating and the potatoes will rot. Inspect the boxes at regular intervals and remove any damaged or rotting tubers.

Varieties

Earlies: 'Duke of York', cream-fleshed and excellent flavour.
'Epicure', renowned for flavour and its deep eyes.
'Sharpe's Express', white-fleshed and good flavour.
'Manna', heavy cropper, good flavour.
'Maris Bard', very early cropper, good flavour.
Maincrop: 'Desirée', cream-fleshed, good flavour, red-skinned, excellent for cooking.
'Kerr's Pink', great quality, floury when cooked.
'Romano', cream-fleshed, good flavour.

RHUBARB

Rhubarb does well in most soils but grows best in rich, lightish soils in an open situation. Whilst it can be grown from seed, it is wise to start with strong, healthy roots planted in March in well-prepared, deeply dug ground, with the crown slightly above the surface. Allow the newly planted rhubarb at least one growing season before starting to take a crop. At no time should the plants be denuded of foliage, which is vital for future health and cropping ability. Be liberal with water in dry weather. During early winter apply a top dressing of well-rotted compost with a follow-up of 'Growmore' fertiliser, 3-4 oz (75-100 g) per plant in February. For an early crop cover an established root or two with a chimney pot or large

Rhubarb 'Victoria'.

wooden box to exclude light, but remove after the first forced rhubarb is pulled.

Varieties
'Timperley Early', 'Victoria', 'Hawke's Champagne'.

SPINACH, NEW ZEALAND SPINACH AND LEAF BEET

Spinach
This widely accepted health food with green leaves reputed to be brimming over with iron and vitamins deserves due attention both from the gardener and the cook. Whilst it will grow on most soils, the ground needs to be fertile and well prepared with the incorporation of some well-rotted compost. On very acid soils, apply garden lime during the previous winter and at the same time 1-2 oz per square yard (25-50 g per m^2) of sulphate of potash.

For summer spinach, plan successional sowings from March, with repeat sowings every two or three weeks until July. This will allow regular picking of the young, succulent leaves. In hot weather the plants tend to bolt to seed, especially if dry at the roots. The rows should be 15 in apart and the seedlings thinned out 3 in apart. When picking starts, take two or three of the largest outside leaves first from each plant. For winter spinach, covering the period October till May, sow again on a successional basis in August and September.

Varieties

'Sigma Leaf' and 'Norvak' for summer cropping. 'Broadleaved Prickly' for November onwards.

Spinach 'Sigma Leaf'.

Swiss chard.

New Zealand Spinach
A totally different plant which rambles and requires much more space. It does best on light to medium soils. Plant outside in May, in sunny position, 3 ft apart. Except for watering in dry weather, little attention is needed. The leaves should be picked when young, singly, by stripping from the stems, which encourages new growth.

Leaf Beet (Swiss Chard or Sea Kale Beet)
Plants with plenty of large foliage and thick leaf stems, the leaves have a similar flavour to the ordinary round leaf spinach; the ribs, cooked separately, have a much milder flavour. For best results, a rich well-drained soil is required to grow and maintain strong plants capable of cropping over a long period. Sow seed outside mid-April in rows 15 in apart, and thin out the seedlings as early as possible to the same distance. The large outside leaves should be removed to keep the plants strong and in continuous leaf growth. Water during hot, dry weather. Cropping will continue well into the autumn, but for better plants during late autumn and early winter a second sowing in July is advisable.

Rhubarb chard, with its long crimson stems and dark foliage, can be grown and cooked in exactly the same way.

81

Planting sweetcorn in blocks ensures cross-pollination.

SWEETCORN

Home-grown corn on the cob is a real treat, and the introduction of early maturing F1 Hybrid varieties offers a good chance of success, despite our unpredictable summer climate. Seed sown in April in a propagating frame needs a temperature of about 55°-60°F (13°-15°C). Use a peat-based compost, and set one seed in each 3 in pot. Choose a sunny sheltered position for outdoor planting under cloches around the third week of May. The ground needs to be well prepared but not overdosed either with compost or manure; too rich a soil makes leaf rather than cobs. Since cob production depends on pollination, set the plants in a square block, 8 in apart each way. Cobs are ready for harvesting when the corn kernels are still soft and milky, but beginning to colour.

Varieties
'First of All', best one for table quality.
'Kelvedon Glory', a good cropper suitable for warmer areas.

TOMATOES

With so many varieties now available for both indoor and outdoor growing, choice of the right one can be something of a lottery. But whereas commercial growers are primarily concerned with cropping capacity, ability to travel, shelf life and eye appeal, the gardener must always go, first and foremost, for flavour.

Greenhouse tomatoes
The plant needs to be compact, with fruit trusses closely spaced on the main stem. In addition the variety must be free from green-back (unripenable green shoul-

ders on the tomatoes), not particularly susceptible to tomato leaf mould, a good cropper capable of early ripening and, above all, have that old-fashioned tomato flavour. Years of trial growing have shown that 'Alicante' comes closest to meeting consistently all these requirements.

Tomatoes require a day temperature of 60°F (16°C), slightly lower at night. Start sowing mid-March, about 30 seeds to each 4 in pot in a peat-based compost, covering them lightly with a little fine compost before watering with a fine rose. In a Ward propagator, with the temperature set at 65°F (18°C), germination occurs within a week. Seedlings can be pricked out into 3½ in as soon as the seed leaves straighten out; from then until planting time they just need careful watering and adequate spacing on the bench to avoid overcrowding and consequent weak growth.

Soil problems

It is safe to plant in virgin greenhouse border soil, but after two or three seasons there may be problems such as verticillium wilt (sleepy disease), etc. Completely changing the soil to a depth of 3 ft every two or three years or chemical sterilisation of the soil are possible answers. However, the use of growing bags or ring culture have been widely accepted as a more practical solution.

Whichever method is used, actively growing plants should be transplanted with plenty of white roots into the final growing medium. Planting two tomatoes per bag, rather than the makers' recommended three or four, gives a higher yield of quality ripe fruits. And a few slits cut with a pocket knife in the sides of the bags well above soil level will obviate the risk of waterlogging.

In ring culture, planting is done in 10 in bottomless bitumised rings or pots filled with John Innes No. 3 compost; these stand on an aggregate base of pea-sized washed gravel, peat or a new product, 'Perlag'. The plants make new roots within the rings and then develop a second set of roots in the aggregate. Water the plants thoroughly after planting and then restrict watering to the aggregate.

With both systems, feeding with a high potash liquid tomato fertiliser starts when the first truss has set and continues at weekly intervals until the end of the cropping season. With ring culture the weekly feeds are applied through the compost in the rings whilst the watering via the aggregate goes on daily as required, according to the weather. Failure to feed regularly results in a poor fruit set and very low yields on the upper trusses. A single watering with lime water (one handful of hydrated lime stirred into 2 gallons (9 litres) of water at the fourth truss stage prevents 'knuckle drop' (flowers breaking from stalks).

Tomatoes in pots

A variety such as 'Alicante', grown in bags or by ring culture, can produce a crop average of 20 lbs (9 kg) per plant. It also does

'Alicante' tomatoes in 8-inch pot.

relatively well in a 8 or 10 in pot, limited to only five trusses per plant. Again using John Innes No. 3 compost, remove the centre growing tip after the formation of the fifth flower truss and use a stout cane for support. Fix a large wooden bead or cotton reel on top of the cane to ensure protection against eye damage when working.

Getting the bottom truss to set when the temperatures are on the low side and the light none too good can be a problem. This can be anticipated and overcome by spraying the open flowers once with a tomato fruit setting spray, 'Betapal', but be careful not to overdose.

To support plants grown on a single stem, use six-ply fillis plus a strand of nylon string for extra strength, essential when the crop weight is at its peak. The string can be fastened round the growing bag or tied to a 12 in metal stake in the ground before it is attached to the top wire. Encouraging the growing plants to climb clockwise round the strings is far simpler than using canes. Growing on single stems produces the best results provided that each and every side shoot is removed when still small. Removal of neglected large side shoots leaves wounds, open to disease and infection.

Essential air circulation around the growing plants is obtained by the opening of both top and side ventilators whenever the weather allows. Better still are automatically operated ventilators set at a required temperature. In cool, damp weather it is a good idea to move the air by using an electric fan. When the bottom truss is fully formed, removal of the leaves below immediately improves air circulation near ground level, reduces the risk of disease and accelerates ripening. Slightly moist air is essential for healthy growth and good fruit set, so during warm weather water the centre path around midday and close the door for a short time. This also reduces the risk of red spider mite. Whitefly can be dealt with by hanging Aeroxon flying insect traps (sticky cards with an incorporated attractant) above the plants. These catch the first few adults and prevent infestation. An alternative is a weekly spray with liquid Derris; in the event of infestation, this will be

Remove tomato side shoots as soon as they appear.

necessary every 2-3 days for about 3 weeks.

Outdoor tomatoes

Even though varieties have been introduced recently that appear to be weather resistant, but to obtain good-quality ripe fruit we are still dealing with plants that need warmth, moisture and lots of sunshine to achieve their full potential. Select, if possible, a full sunshine position, sheltered by a wall or fence where the soil has been well prepared but not too richly built up either with compost or manure. Excessive fertility results in masses of leaves and slow fruit ripening. Better still, plant in growing bags or pots on the patio or on the path along the south side of the house. The bush variety 'Tornado' now leads the field;

planted end of May, it will be loaded with bright red tomatoes full of flavour in July and August. 'Alicante' and 'Golden Sunrise' can also be grown successfully in bags and pots outside, using the same technique as for cultivating in pots under glass.

TURNIPS, SWEDES AND CHICORY

Turnips

As members of the brassica family, turnips should be fitted accordingly into the crop rotation scheme, to minimise the risk of club root. An early crop can be grown from seed sown in March in a cold frame or under cloches. For this 'Milan White' is a suitable variety. Turnips are fast growing so if seed is sown outdoors in April in a sunny situation the crop will be ready in June. Sow in ¾in deep drills in a well-prepared seed-bed that has recently been given a light dressing of garden lime. To avoid flea beetle damage in a dry spring, treat the emerging seedlings with Derris dust and repeat again after thinning out the seedlings 6 in apart. Successional sowings in rows 12 in apart every few weeks throughout the summer until August will maintain a continuous supply of tender turnips. Do not allow them to get old as they become tough and coarse.

Varieties

'Milan White', for the early crop under cover.
'Snowball', quick growing early

white with mild flavour.
'Golden Ball', sown in June or July, is a good keeper, juicy and sweet.

Swedes

Hardier and milder in flavour than turnips, but more difficult to grow in a small garden or on an allotment, mainly because of mildew. The risk can be reduced by delaying sowing until May, but even so a preventive fungicide application of Supercarb (Carbendazin) in late August is advisable.

Sowing procedure is as for turnips but thin out to 12 in apart so that each plant stands free of its partners in the row. At the end of the growing season, swedes tend to keep better when left in the ground, rather than lifted and stored. The best variety for the small garden is 'Marian', which has superseded the older and more mildew susceptible varieties.

Chicory

Chicory chicons have long been a popular winter vegetable on the continent both as a luxury winter salad or as a cooked vegetable. After a tentative start, growing chicory has become a regular crop in our vegetable garden. Prepare the ground as for most other root crops, but avoid the use of either fresh manure or compost as recent applications produce forked roots, whereas straight roots something akin to thin parsnips are wanted for forcing. Deep digging is beneficial plus 2-3 oz (50- 80 g) of 'Growmore' fertiliser worked in when the seed-bed is prepared.

Sow early in June in a shallow drill in rows 12 in apart and thin out the seedlings as soon as practicable to 8 in apart. Lift the roots for forcing in October, trimming the tops cleanly just above the crown before planting them in a row in front of a south-facing fence. Then with the crowns 2-3 in down, heap 6-8 in of home-made compost on top in a ridge. During late winter or early spring every root will produce a superb chicon.

One of the best varieties for forcing is 'Witloof Zoom' (Brussels chicory).

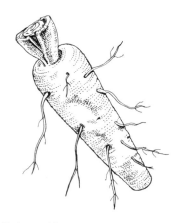

To force chicory, shorten the lifted roots and trim off the tops.

17. HERBS

A small area of the garden should be set aside for a selection of the more frequently used culinary herbs. Even if space cannot be found for all of them, most will do well in pots and troughs placed close by the kitchen door. Smaller containers make it easier for them to be transferred to a cold greenhouse in winter, where they continue to grow slowly but well enough to replace the regular removal of the pieces of fresh foliage needed in the kitchen. Many herbs can be grown from seed but it is preferable to start with either a well-rooted healthy plant or a cutting from a good stock plant.

Bay Laurel (*Laurus nobilis*). Whilst a bay tree can be grown successfully in a large pot or tub, ideally it needs space outside in

the open ground and can be an attractive addition to the shrub border. In a severe winter, plants in tubs or pots can be killed if the soil in the container freezes solidly. Propagation is from semi-mature shoots prepared as cuttings about 4 in long, in August, for rooting either in a cold frame or greenhouse. The leaves, fresh or dried, can be used in soups, stews, etc.

Borage (*Borago officinalis*). A hardy annual plant that thrives anywhere. Start with seed sown outside early May, thin out the

A corner of herb garden.

Borage.

seedlings to 15 in apart and you will have a delightful display of blue flowers in July. Allowing a few to set seed ensures a good supply of borage in the garden. The leaves are used in pickles and salads or as an addition to fruit juices and the flowers in claret cups or crystallised as cake decoration.

Chives (*Allium schoenoprasum*). A hardy perennial, propagated by division of the roots in spring or autumn, which can be grown from seed. Lift and divide clumps every three or four years. Its thin onion-like foliage is used for flavouring salads, tomato dishes and omelettes. Although the flowers are attractive, they reduce the leaf growth if left to die on the plants.

Fennel (*Foeniculum officinale*). A single plant of this hardy perennial is certainly sufficient. Grown from seed sown in spring, it grows to a height of 6-7 ft , so it is not suitable for a container. It has aniseed flavour and is mostly used in fish dishes. 'Florence Fennel', an Italian bred variety, is an annual which produces large, white, solid bulbs, used as a vegetable.

Garlic (*Allium sativum*). In March plant the small cloves of garlic bulbs in 3 in pots in a cold greenhouse and bring them into growth; plant out in early May 6 in apart, and earth up regularly during the growing period. Garlic likes well drained soil and a sunny position. Harvest the bulbs when the foliage has died down naturally. String the bulbs together and store in a dry frost-free place. The culinary uses are legion, from strong flavoured dishes to scenting a salad bowl.

Mint (*Mentha*). This popular garden herb, propagated by root division in March, succeeds best in loamy soils with plenty of moisture. The common form is *Mentha spicata* but the round-leaved *Mentha rotundifolia* (sometimes known as apple mint or Bowles mint) has a better flavour. The roots are very invasive but this can be overcome by planting inside a sunken bottom-less container. A few bits of root planted in a pot and kept over the winter in a cold greenhouse will supply some very early mint for the kitchen before the plants outside come into growth. The leaves are used fresh or dried in numerous ways, notably for mint sauce and mint jelly.

Parsley This herb is used for flavouring as well as for decoration of dishes. When the soil is warm, it can be sown outdoors, but sown early April in a propagating frame, germination is fairly quick at a temperature of 60°-64°F (15°-17°C). Prick out into individual 3 in pots and plant out towards end May. A second sowing in small pots will give fresh parsley in the greenhouse or on the windowsill all through the winter.

Rosemary (*Rosmarinus officinalis*). A hardy evergreen shrub (although an exceptional hard frost may kill it), very suitable for growing in a medium-sized container. Cuttings of 6 in taken during the summer root easily in a slightly shady border or in a pot kept under the greenhouse bench. The leaves are used fresh or dried with meat, or for making rosemary tea.

Sage (*Salvia officinalis*). This low-growing perennial shrub is best propagated from cuttings taken from non-flowering plants early in the summer. Raised from seed, the plants flower too freely and the leaves are of lower quality. There are green-leaved and purple-leaved forms, the

Purple and green sage.

latter a good plant for the ornamental border. Both do best in warm dryish situations, and are completely hardy. The leaves can be used either fresh or dried in stuffing and with fatty meats.

Thyme (*Thymus vulgaris*).
Lemon scented thyme (*Thymus citrodorus*). Both can be propagated from 3 in cuttings taken with a heel during the summer. As the shoots often root into the surrounding soil, it is possible to take an Irish cutting (cuttings with the roots already formed). The plants get very straggly, so cut back old specimens drastically early in the year and replace completely every three years. The leaves are used for seasoning meat dishes and in stuffing.

INDEX